A RATIONALIST MANIFESTO

Just Another Little Book to Save the World

Colin Costa

I0462038

A RATIONALIST MANIFESTO

Copyright © Colin Costa 2019

Earth image from free stock photos
at www.pexels.com

Published by Richard Guise

Printed by www.lulu.com

ISBN: 978-0-244-75160-9

To the friends whose

comments, criticisms and questions

have helped me form these ideas.

A Rationalist Manifesto

Contents

An Alien's View

It seems highly unlikely that any intelligent life from beyond our planet will visit us in the forseeable future, if ever. The distances are just too great. But if it did so in the present day, what would it find?

A planet teeming with life adapted to the extremes of Earth's environment. A planet whose land surface is dominated by one intelligent species, but a species among the *least* adapted to the natural environments in which it chooses to live. Instead, humans have adapted their environment to suit themselves, even surviving for short periods on and under the seas, in the air and in the immediate neighbourhood of the local star system. This they've achieved by rational scientific research into their own biology and into the physical world around and beyond them.

And yet many humans benefit little from the discoveries and achievements of the few. Some barely survive childhood. Some don't even do that. Over ten per cent are undernourished[*]. A similar proportion are without clean drinking water. About twenty per cent have no access to one of the most basic discoveries of the last two centuries:

---

[*] Sources of statistics can be found in the 'References' section towards the end of this book.

electricity. Just as many have inadequate housing – or even no home at all – and some of these live in the wealthiest areas of the planet.

Humans have a remarkable talent for destroying their own environment – and themselves. At the time of writing, humans are killing each other in fifteen separate wars. The most destructive weapons yet invented by the ever-resourceful *homo sapiens* were first deployed over seventy years ago. Since then, despite the constantly declared objective of decommissioning all of them, their numbers – and the number of organisations capable of using them – have grown such that there are now estimated to be about 15,000 nuclear weapons around the planet. Quite apart from the barely imaginable destruction, each can kill millions of people. The current world population is about 7,500,000,000. Do the maths.

Our alien would inevitably conclude that humans live on a fragile planet, made more fragile by their own behaviour. What, the alien might well ask, are they doing about it? How are they organised to tackle the problems of their planet and their own species in particular?

The answers are, respectively, not a lot and not at all.

Education hasn't guaranteed enlightenment. Information hasn't improved intelligence. In the best educated and best informed countries, millions of humans spend much of their time gawping at mass 'entertainment', listening to the wails and shrieks of juvenile millionaires, praying to non-existent gods or simply drinking or doping themselves to an early exit.

This little book doesn't have all the solutions to the world's problems. It's not an ecological or psychological manual. It's a list of principles that I believe to be right and which, I suggest, need to be accepted in order to allow human beings to start solving more problems than they create. Some of them you may find surprising. I have no talent for politics or leadership and in any case am too old. It's my hope that at least someone with such talent may read this.

In many cases the context is the UK and Europe, on which my general ignorance is less than elsewhere, but I've tried to express the principles in a way that's generally applicable.

CC, 2019

Out With The Old

There Is No God. Full Stop.

Can six billion people be wrong? You bet they can. Until about five hundred years ago almost every human believed the sun and stars revolved around the Earth.

You don't even need any scientific knowledge to demonstrate that at least four billion of the six billion present-day humans who claim to believe in god are wrong. Simple logic will do. About two billion Christians believe there's just one god – and it's the one whose son is Jesus and who had nothing special to do with an Arabian named Mohammed born five hundred years after Jesus's death. Some one and a half billion Muslims believe it's the one who revealed himself to Mohammed. A billion Hindus think there are hundreds of gods, none of which is either the Christians' or the Muslims' version. Another one and a half billion deny all of these but believe in some other deity or other. If any are right, the others are wrong. So the least that could possibly be wrong is four billion.

In fact the numbers don't matter, because they're all wrong. This isn't arrogance – the evidence speaks for itself. Gods are human creations, not the other way around. The Christian Bible has a lot to say about the plight of Jews in the Middle East and how people should behave in the day-to-day life of first-century Palestine, but not so much on how the contemporary native people of South America, for example, should run their lives. You may argue the principles apply universally, but I'm not aware of any other divine representative from God having turned up in the Andes to pass them on. Rather an oversight on the part of an omnipresent, omniscient being. Could a relevant fact be that one region of human communities was unknown to the other? Likewise, it surely can't be just coincidence that Islam focuses on the very same suppressive view of women that also occupied the minds of Arabian men at the time Mohammed reported what he claimed to be the word of a timeless and universal god. Pull the other one. And, as if circumstantial evidence weren't enough, you could always go to India, where they're quite honest about inventing their gods. While on a tour of Kolkata and interrogating our guide about the Hindu religion, I was surprised to learn that a god of computers had recently been announced. (And if I could remember the god's name, I'd be tempted to call on his or her help whenever Microsoft sends my laptop into a trance.)

Given the overwhelming evidence that no god or gods really exist – and the complete lack of any proper evidence to the contrary – one of the modern world's great mysteries is why so many well-educated, well-read and otherwise intelligent people still believe they do. Or is it such a mystery? While we're all born with a blank cultural slate, it's not long before most of us are told in no uncertain terms what we're supposed to believe in, shortly followed by a hint of the dire consequences of our failing to toe the line. Any child of an average Taoist Chinese family would, if moved as an infant to an average Texan family, grow up a Christian. Culture rules. It takes quite an effort to ditch long-held beliefs, especially when everyone around you still seems to hold them. You can forgive the weak or those with little access to objective education for holding onto the faith of their parents. It's harder to forgive those who've benefited from a liberal, Western education. (And yet, of course, in some cases we should: friendship trumps religion.)

The third-worst offenders are the intellectually bright clerics who, having failed to recognise their own beliefs as fairy tales, proceed to support others in the same delusions. The second-worst are missionaries who go one step further and try to persuade those who'd previously escaped their world view, especially those with less confidence and learning than themselves, to sign up to their nonsense. But at the absolute bottom of the moral and intellectual pit lie those who preach an attitude to religion that gained traction in the twentieth century and today has an invidious influence on too many politicians of a liberal bent. These are the cultural relativists.

If I understand it correctly (and so weird is their stance it seems wise to add this caveat), a cultural relativist declares that whatever the people of a particular culture believe, it's true *for them*. Hindus believe in reincarnation, so it must be true. People on the Pacific island of Tanna believe Prince Philip is a god, so it must be true. While all religious believers are deluded, cultural relativists must be literally insane. The consequence of their philosophy – or perhaps its cause – is the modern cult of respect (of which more later). We're all supposed to respect everyone else – *and their beliefs*. This is, quite literally, madness. If I visited Tanna, I suspect I'd have a lot of respect for many of the people there, but you want me to respect their delusion that a funny, exasperating, charming, tax-guzzling and all-too-human resident of Berkshire is a living deity (or, probably by the time you read this, a deceased deity)? No chance.

Grow up, world. Gods were something humans invented after they got creativity and before they got science. It's over. Drop it. If some of you can't drop it, then at least let the rest of us ignore you. Sit quietly in your gardens and pray to Prince Philip or the Tooth Fairy or Bonko the God of Blu-Tack. Just don't bother anyone else about it. And certainly don't get involved in managing the world.

PRINCIPLE 1: Gods are fiction[*].

PRINCIPLE 2: Government should ignore religion and spend no money supporting it.

Although it's probably not necessary, here are a few examples of how and where Principle 2 is *not* currently in operation:

- The very first article of the constitution of Saudi Arabia states that 'the Kingdom of Saudi Arabia is a sovereign Arab *Islamic* State'.
- Indonesia's constitution, adopted in 1945 and as revised in 2002, states that '*by the grace of God Almighty* ... the people of Indonesia hereby declare their

---

[*] A list of all thirteen principles can be found towards the end of this book.

independence'.

- Pakistan's constitution opens with the following astonishing caveat: 'Whereas *sovereignty over the entire Universe belongs to Almighty Allah alone*, and the authority to be exercised by the people of Pakistan within the limits prescribed by Him is a sacred trust...'
- The UK's House of Lords still includes twenty-six members appointed simply because they're bishops in the Church of England.
- The British state not only still permits the existence of faith schools but also grants them the financially advantageous status of a charity.

It doesn't have to be like this. Many European countries separate state and religion, either partially or completely. Even in the USA, where atheists are regarded with the same suspicion as communists, a presidential candidate may have any – or no – religion... even though, you might add, no non-Christian would stand a chance. Another surprising beacon of rationality, in this respect at least, is the constitution of Israel (hardly a bastion of liberalism), by which both rabbis and ministers of any other religion are specifically banned from standing for parliament.

You see, these things are not impossible. Such common sense prompts a wider principle:

PRINCIPLE 3: Any individual declaring belief in the supernatural should be barred from public office.

What Is Government For?

We've already mentioned things governments are doing but shouldn't, and things they should be doing but aren't. This is all a matter of opinion. Isn't it strange, then, that rarely – if ever – are electorates asked what they think their government should and should not be involved in, let alone what their objectives and priorities should be? Yes, election manifestos are full of what one party or another proposes to prioritise. 'Education, education, education.' (That's fairly clear.) 'Health and social mobility are our top priorities.' (You can't have two at the top, mate.) 'Our number-one goal is to defend our citizens against the forces of evil.' (So why did you spend that money on a symphony orchestra instead of some extra police officers?) No, outside of revolutions, the vast majority of a new government's activities turn out to be simply the continuation of the old government's, with a little change of emphasis here and there, accompanied by plenty of press releases.

So what *is* government for? Centuries ago it was just to accumulate wealth and wage war. (*Plus ça change*, a cynic may say.) Nowadays, in many countries, it seems to be to fund the life of every citizen from the cradle to the grave. Correction: from nine months before the cradle. To ask the same question another way, what do taxpayers think their taxes should be spent on? Or, more pertinently, *not* be spent on?

Here's one person's opinion. It happens to be mine, but anyone else could come up with their own list – the point being that, while everyone would indeed have an opinion, governments seem peculiarly uninterested in asking for them. Suspiciously uninterested.

*

(In this section, by 'taxes', I mean compulsory taxation rather than voluntary sources of public funds such as lotteries or donations.)

Taxes should pay for essential services. Let's call them **List A**. They include:

- Security
- Emergency services
- Justice
- Health care
- Education
- Networked utilities
- Transport infrastructure
- Environmental protection
- Scientific research
- Democratic processes

- Support for those unable to support themselves

Taxes should *not* pay for **List B**: non-essential activities. These include:

- Sport
- Art
- Music
- Libraries
- Other cultural activities
- Space exploration
- State visits
- Other public ceremonies

Is the cat satisfactorily among the pigeons? The point is not that people will disagree with the content of the lists, but that most will surely agree that there *are* two lists: one to be funded by compulsory taxation and one not.

Whatever appears in List B would still carry on, of course. People would still want to listen to opera and celebrate festivals. So, where they require common expenditure, how could List B activities be funded, if not from compulsory taxation? Well, where practical, like any other product: from sales. Where less practical, from non-compulsory taxation. Take sport. In many countries, huge amounts of public money are spent on facilities for training athletes and delivering them to international events to represent their country.

The extreme physical exercise is certainly not essential for the athletes' health. So what's the point? Apparently it's so that their co-patriots, lounging at home in front of the TV, can get some pleasure from cheering them on and, should they happen to win, feeling vicarious pride in their achievements. Nothing objectionable in that perhaps – except that those who aren't interested shouldn't be forced to contribute to what is clearly a non-essential service. If the football World Cup and the Olympic Games never took place again, the globe would still keep turning and no one would die as a result. So isn't it obvious they should be funded by voluntary contributions? Hooked on the Olympics? So subscribe to a National Sports Fund. An NSF would not be part of any government, and its priorities (basketball over diving, for example) would be determined by its paying members rather than by government committee. Likewise symphony orchestras or missions to Mars (Personally, I'd voluntarily contribute to the Mars missions.) We'll come back to Lists A and B later.

Note that the sample lists above make no mention of 'foreign' relations or 'international' development, since there's no assumption of the geographical level at which any of these services may be managed. This topic will be covered later as well. For the moment, here's the proposed principle:

> PRINCIPLE 4: Government funded by compulsory taxation should supply only those services deemed essential by a clear majority of the taxpayers.

The Absurd Economic Objective

One thing that probably most people – and certainly most politicians – think is the business of government is managing the economy. Some even think it the most important: 'Get the economy right [and by this they mean their national economy] and everything else will fall into place.' But what is 'right'? This leads to one of the most absurd objectives our alien is likely to come across.

Never have so many people been in such thrall to such an insignificant statistic. We hear it all the time:

- This government will focus relentlessly on growth.
- The economy has fallen by 0.2%. We're still in recession!
- China is growing by 9%. Why can't we?
- Look at the year-on-year trend – we could be headed for a double-dip!
- The Bank of England has slashed the growth forecast – it may be another year before the economy's moving again!

The exclamation marks are not gratuitous. People really do get so worked up about this 'growth' business that they speak in exclamation marks. They probably think in exclamation marks. When news of a low growth rate or even, heaven forbid, a negative growth rate hits the airwaves, you'd think a meteor was headed our way and we'd got just half an hour to live.

Growth of what? Why do they think it matters? Do they even know what or why?

As referred to *ad nauseam* by economists, politicians, journalists and the like, 'growth' means a positive change in gross domestic product (GDP). GDP itself is supposed to be the total value of all consumption, investment and government spending in a country within a period (usually a year), plus the difference between exports (which push it up) and imports (which pull it down). In Britain the growth statistic that hits the airwaves most often is the change in the UK's GDP per quarter, duly adjusted for predictable seasonal changes.

So if in the last three months you've bought a car (or, for that matter, a box of matches) *and* that purchase increased your spending compared to the previous three months *and* you bought it from someone who's liable for income tax in the UK, then you've contributed – in however small a way – to the economic growth figure announced with such ponderous gravity. The wizards of Westminster take it for granted that this must be a good thing. And why? It's a shame that interviewers so rarely ask politicians this very question: why is any increase in GDP a good thing? I suspect a fair number would struggle to explain the reason. I suspect, in fact, that a fair number have not even bothered to ponder the reason: the party leader says growth is good, the economic gurus say growth is good, the speech writers say growth is good... and so growth must be good. End of story.

If anyone thinks about it at all, they must think something along the lines of 'Well, last quarter you didn't buy a car and this quarter you did – and if that's the only difference between the two totals, not only must you be happier (or else you wouldn't have bought the car) but also the dealer who sold it must be happier. No one loses. Growth is good. Amen.'

But behind such thoughts lurks a big assumption, doesn't it? An assumption big enough to be the elephantine assumption in the room. What if one more person were born during the quarter, while no one died? The higher GDP is now divided between more people than the lower one and, while you and the car dealer may be happier, on average everyone else has a lower GDP – and is therefore, by parallel assumption, unhappier. The elephant is population growth. So if total

GDP grows, it would have to grow faster than population does for GDP *per person* – effectively average income – to increase. And isn't that what the growth fans actually mean? Isn't growing average incomes what they actually want? Well, if it is, they seem peculiarly shy about saying it. And if it isn't – well, going back to where we started – what's the point of a rising total GDP?

But even if the statistic reflected what they want, economic growth is still an absurd objective, and the number of people pointing this out in the last fifty years must now be in the millions. The list of costs generated by increased consumption – costs that don't appear in any negative row at the end of the GDP sum – grows by the day: noise, pollution, stress, accidents, depletion of finite resources, destruction of natural habitats... it's old hat, but it's as true as ever. One irony is that many practical measures taken to alleviate these side-effects, be they the sale of catalytic converters, ear-defenders or badger tunnels, actually *add* to GDP (and therefore, according to most governments' economic assumptions, to happiness) each time the cash register rings. Other absurdities are even more direct. Buying ingredients to make a terrorist bomb? Thank you, sir. Kerr-ching! More happiness. Upgrading nuclear weapons to kill more innocent people more effectively? Sign here, sir. Kerr-ching! More happiness.

So bad is measured as good. Even Orwell would have thought this too absurd to be conceivable.

PRINCIPLE 5: Economic growth, as an isolated aggregate statistic, should be dropped from all government analysis.

Nation Does Not Equal State

Here's a simple and obvious notion. And, if only politicians could accommodate it in their vast but cluttered brains, a good deal of the world's angst and violence would be avoided. Here it comes:

PRINCIPLE 6: 'Nation' and 'State' are two different things and should be treated as such.

A *nation* is a *cultural* entity, distinguished from other nations by a subset of language, history, music, religion and so on. A *state* is an *administrative* entity, distinguished from other states by its legal jurisdiction – and by that alone.

While location or residence in a particular state is an objective fact, location in or membership of a nation is often a matter of opinion. Residents of Tarragona in Spain are definitely in the state of Spain (or were at the time of writing). Whether they're in the nation of Spain or the nation of Catalonia, or both or neither, is a matter of opinion or sometimes preference.

For some strange reason – and I blame the 1648 Treaty of Westphalia – people have got it into their heads that any nation has the right to be a state. This bizarre and dangerous idea has some sway at the United Nations (which is actually a union of states, but the title 'United States' had already been taken). Croatia was a nation, so it became a state. Ditto Bosnia, Slovakia, Estonia and all the rest.

And why is this dangerous? Because states have power and nations generate the emotion to misuse it. Take the Falklands / Las Malvinas. A majority in the nation of Britain, being infused with notions of superiority and imperialism, thinks the islands should 'belong to' Britain. A majority in the nation of Argentina, being infused with notions of inferiority and posturing, thinks they should 'belong to' Argentina. This should have been a simple matter for the UN to resolve but, alas, in 1982 Britain and Argentina were not only nations but also states, both with control over the deployment of military forces. The nations drove the states to invade. Chaos and disaster followed and many lives were lost. The point is that nations should be positively *discouraged* from becoming states. States, as with all administrations, should run on rationality not nationality. Nations, by their very nature, are fuelled by emotion. The two don't mix.

PRINCIPLE 7: The nation-state is a bad thing.

To our intelligent alien, this would be a self-evident conclusion from the briefest study of post-medieval Earth history. To secure for their nation-state lucrative trade deals, supplies of natural resources, strategic outposts, more territory or simply prestige, national leaders have ordered troops under their command to slaughter millions who happened to be born into another state. Infused with allegiance to the nation (as opposed to state), the military has obeyed. Similarly driven, the citizens at home have largely urged them on. Even today the ultimate defence of any policy by any national politician is to claim it protects their own citizens. Implication: and to hell with any other citizens. Such a blinkered view of the world is the inevitable consequence of power being concentrated at the level of the nation-state: the mandate of those in power is a national one and therefore their mindset is a national one.

(It's an unfortunate feature of English and other languages that the adjective from both 'nation' and 'state' is 'national'. There's no such word as 'statal'. 'Statist', like 'nationalist', means something else. Nor does it help that 'state' is used to refer to sub-national entities in, for example, the USA and Germany, as well as to the larger entity. Language is a powerful tool, especially when operating subconsciously. It's easy to assume that, because the description 'national' is applied to, say, a parliament, the geographical entity it represents is a single 'nation'. The obvious example where this is not the case is Russia, a state of several nations. You could argue the same for the UK or Spain, but less clearly in both cases, since the larger unit has had enough shared history and generates enough emotional allegiance of its own to claim nationhood as well. Nations overlap; states do not.)

If our alien were to turn from history to geography, he'd probably find the distribution of states – the 200-odd entities in which sovereign power is traditionally concentrated – so absurd he'd remove his little alien reading glasses and give them a good clean. Some states appear to swallow up over half a continent's worth of territory, while others are so small they're virtually lost inside the width of a frontier marked on a map. Leaving aside debatable little quirks like Monaco and the Vatican City, the status of 'sovereign state' applies just the same to the 10,000,000 square kilometres of Canada as to the Pacific island group of Tuvalu, whose land territory would fit about 16 times into the city of Montreal alone. The entire territory of the EU's 28 states (at the time of writing) could fit inside Russia nearly four times. A citizen of Belize is one of a few hundred thousand, while a Chinese citizen shares her status with some one and a half *billion* others.

In terms of political influence the scales are even more lop-sided. The UK, a relatively minor state in both population and area, holds one of the five permanent seats on the UN's fifteen-strong Security Council, and can thereby veto any substantive resolution. Brazil, over thirty times as big and home to over three times as many people, is currently not even one of the non-permanent members. Nor are many other candidates more obvious than the UK or France. The 'Great Powers', as they used to be called – apparently without any embarrassment – still claim 'spheres of influence' (Russia over the Middle East, the USA over Latin America and so on), as though these in some way represented an inalienable right.

Yet more bizarre is the continued existence of what are effectively still colonies of former imperial powers, not only territorially detached but often thousands of kilometres from their 'home' country: Saint Pierre and

Miquelon (French), Anguilla and Gibraltar (British), Ceuta and Melilla (Spanish) and many more. The argument that a majority of their residents may want to retain their status as far-flung citizens of a former empire merely reflects their historical allegiances, which – and this is the essence of the argument here – is an irrational basis on which to organise a territory's administration. For 'irrational', read 'wrong'. Just imagine if the majority of residents in those eastern districts of Leicester dominated by ethnically Indian people, voted to be administered not as an English local government unit, but as an Indian overseas territory. If you think that's absurd, then you must think likewise of the political status of Gibraltar, the Falklands, New Caledonia and the rest. The fact that the United Nations supports the 'right' of 'self-determination', as it calls it, doesn't make the situation any less absurd. Are irrational historical legacies – and the tensions they generate – to be left festering forever? If so, why not hand Britannia and Gaul back to the Romans?

(In fact the UN reference is to 'respect for the principle of equal rights and self-determination of peoples'. Note: peoples, not people. What on earth is a people? A nation, a religion, a race, some other ethnic group? What if they live cheek by jowl with another 'people'? Who are the 'selves' that are allowed to determine their governance? It's a legalistic shambles that should be either rewritten or removed from the UN Charter. Preferably the latter.)

Some readers may be bristling at my 'unpatriotic' suggestions of breaking old colonial ties and may be muttering to themselves something along the lines of 'Government and politics are more than mere logic. We aren't robots, we're human beings with histories, cultures and allegiances. What's wrong with having friends on the other side of the world? Hands across the sea and all that.'

Well, there's nothing wrong with 'all that'. Everyone is indeed the product of a particular culture (or cultures) and most feel a strong allegiance to their 'tribe', be it nation, religion, ethnic group or whatever – and they probably live in a territory dominated by the same 'tribe'.

But here's the point. There are plenty of outlets for expressing such allegiances – sport, music, theatre, art, ritual, ceremony, flag-waving festivals and the rest – that do not impinge on the practical, day-to-day governance of a region and its people. So why not restrict the application of national allegiance to these safe areas, rather than let it infect the rather boring, but rather powerful, world of public administration?

> PRINCIPLE 8: A system of public
> administration conceived, structured and
> run without the baggage of national identity
> and allegiance is a safer system.

*

And how might the remaining, restricted activities, expressing national allegiance, be organised? This rings a bell. They are, of course, classic 'List B' activities, as suggested under 'What Is Government For?' These are non-essential activities that appeal to some citizens but not others. Number one on this list comes next...

The King Is Dead. Full Stop.

Hereditary monarchs have been around for thousands of years, whether called kings, queens, chiefs, pharaohs, emperors, empresses or whatever, and whether thought to be the embodiment of god or mere mortals. The tribes, nations or empires at whose head they've stood have varied from the smallest corner of the remotest territory to a swathe of the Earth's surface on which the sun never set.

One thing these monarchs all have in common, however, is that if they've qualified for the job on merit this has been pure coincidence. Another is that – in almost all cases – they're history. Of today's 200 or so states, just 43 have a monarch at their head. Of these, 38 are constitutional or semi-constitutional monarchies, where either the monarch's power is severely restricted, their roles are totally ceremonial or they are actually elected. The five others are Brunei, Oman, Saudi Arabia, Swaziland and the United Arab Emirates. These are home to about 50 million people, i.e. less than one per cent of the Earth's population. I think it's fair to say that monarchy, as a practical system of running a country, is on the way out. Virtually out of the door in fact. Which is a good thing, of course. This is the twenty-first century after all and surely the days of those mostly Middle-Eastern throwbacks are numbered.

But what of the remaining constitutional monarchies, where monarchs are still enthroned but do barely anything useful? The obvious example is, of course, the British version, responsible for the system's survival in no less than 16 of the 38 states. At the time of writing Elizabeth II is still in place, but we have the bizarre situation where many of her 'subjects', including many in the UK, say that when she dies their support for the monarchy would die with her. You have to wonder how firm a grasp these people have on the essential attribute of a system they claim to support: that it's hereditary, which is to say you get whoever's next in line – whether you like them or not, whether they're sufficiently 'majesterial' or not, or indeed whether they're sane or not.

In the unfortunate circumstance that such monarchies survive, they are clear candidates for 'List B': those public services which, however much passion and support they glean from those of a patriotic persuasion, are not essential to the practicalities of government. They are quintessentially 'national' phenomena rather than state departments. Their rules and regalia, their palaces, processions and paraphernalia, as well as their their special security requirements, should all be funded only by those who derive some pleasure from this kind of thing. I'm sure a 'British Monarchy Club' would attract plenty of subscribers – overseas subscriptions welcome, I assume. If not... well, who cares? As far as government would be concerned, the king is dead. Full stop.

> PRINCIPLE 9: Monarchies should be definitively removed from the business of government and any that remain should not be funded by compulsory taxation.

There's No Such Thing As Independence

In September 2003 fifty million Italians were left with no electricity. The blackout was eventually traced to a minor accident on a power line in Switzerland. In 2014, after Russia annexed Crimea, the Ukrainian government ordered the shutdown of the peninsula's vital water supply channel, sourced elsewhere in Ukraine, creating widespread water shortages in the dry south of Crimea, which continue to this day.

With apologies for repetition, this is the twenty-first century. The world is interconnected. No country is independent, nor can it be. There's no such thing as Scottish independence. Nor, for that matter, British, Spanish, Russian or Brazilian independence. Independence for Catalonia? Dream on.

Let's get one thing straight: the Earth is a single planet on which we all depend. When in April 1986 an accident occurred at the Chernobyl nuclear plant in northern Ukraine, the fall-out didn't screech to a halt at the Ukrainian border. When in 2007 a crisis developed in the US sub-prime mortgage market, the repercussions reverberated around the world. The government of almost every country (or actually every country) depends on computer systems. How many of these countries could replace them by equipment manufactured on their own territory? Very few. How many of those who could would be able to supply the rare metals used to build them? Hardly any. Or none. The only way any country could be independent is to strap a rocket to its sturdiest point and blast itself out of Earth orbit. Independence is a myth left over from the days when everything beyond your nearest hill lay in territory called The Unknown.

PRINCIPLE 10: There's no such thing as an independent state.

So why do people celebrate 'independence' days? Why have nations that aren't states, such as Catalonia or Scotland, characterised their efforts to become a state as a 'struggle for independence'? (Or, even more absurdly, 'for freedom'?) The question posed to the Scottish electorate in 2014 was "Should Scotland be an independent country?" Perhaps they should have added in brackets "by blasting itself off into space".

All this nonsense is caused by another instance of simple linguistic confusion. What they're talking about isn't independence at all, but political sovereignty. What they want to have (or, of course, don't want to have) is a regional government above which there is no legal jurisdiction. But that phrase isn't sexy enough, is it? No one but lawyers is interested in 'legal jurisdiction'. Which is a shame, because that's exactly what seems to get so many people hot under the collar: legal jurisdiction on immigration rules or drone attacks or fishing rights or Sharia law or bombing campaigns or goodness knows what else.

Legal jurisdiction also happens to be what much of this book is about, so let's try and make the concept a bit sexier by considering another principle that should put another cat among those flapping pigeons...

This Land Is Not Our Land

It was Woody Guthrie who in 1940 wrote the lyrics 'This land is your land, this land is our land.' The land he was referring to was the United States of America.

But the territory over which the USA currently has legal jurisdiction existed for millions of years before any human set foot on it, for a few thousand more before any European did and will still exist after Americans, native or otherwise, have ceased to inhabit the planet. To characterise it as 'our land', or indeed anybody's land, can be only a temporary claim.

Political land ownership (as opposed to private land ownership, which we'll touch on later) is a subject that generates strong passions. When English people hear the word 'England', they may well visualise a landscape of rolling hills and hedgerows, a corner of the world 'that is forever England'. But it hasn't been of course. It's been Mercia or the Danelaw or the Roman province of Britannia or the land of the Coritani. Tribes come and go, but the territory is there much longer. Empires expand and contract, but the same rivers still generally flow through the same valleys. Our alien would think it bizarre that each generation living on each patch of the Earth's surface should think it ought to belong to their 'tribe', always and forever. And as to the tribe's claim to the airspace above it and thousands of square kilometres of sea beyond its shores, inhabited only by fish... well, alien words would fail him.

So here's another principle in the offing – and one that many people might find the hardest to swallow:

PRINCIPLE 11: No part of the Earth, be it land, sea or air, belongs to any nation, state, race or tribe.

The Party's Over

The dictionary defines a political party as a group of people sharing a common political aim. What could be wrong with that?

How long have you got?

First, whatever the laudable motivation that brought any party into existence, it's almost certain that after a few years its prime – if unwritten – objective will have become its own survival and expansion. In the case of a political party in power, its prime objective is to stay in power. For a party not in power, its prime objective is to get into power. In order to achieve these aims, all other considerations – including any residual concern for its original purpose, such as 'uniting the nation' or 'representing the working classes' – are quietly pushed to the background, at least by those actually running the party. The question 'Will this policy win us votes?' is likely to carry much more weight than 'Is this policy in line with our ideals?'

Second, the motivation of a party's elected members is also questionable. Originally they may well have been as varied as those of any group of people: justice, compassion, greed, fame, desire to be liked, lust for power and so on. After a while, however, their personal objectives will have become submerged under the already-corrupted objective of the party that got them elected or they will have resigned or been removed. The organisation always wins.

Third, how do political parties fare in their supposed role (at least in a liberal democracy) as a channel for bringing the wishes of the electorate to fruition in government policy? In many case, rather poorly. In a single election, different parties present different bundles of policy suggestions to the public. Voters duly cast their votes. But what does each vote reveal about that person's view on any one policy? Nothing. Zilch. No one but the voter knows why they put their X against Mr Nookiberger of the National Party, rather than Ms Pocklington of the People's Party or Mr Dubois of the Democrats or indeed independent candidate Ms Inkspot. Was it because of the National Party's policy A, B, C or Z? Because the voter rather liked Mr N's hairstyle and *despite* his party's policies? Or because Pocklington, Dubois and Inkspot all campaigned against the voter's application to open a lap-dancing club on the high street? Or maybe the voter didn't even know any of the candidates, but was rather taken by the background music in the National Party's TV broadcast? Or was it simply a random vote against the previous government. Who knows?

The existence of competing political parties is touted as a beacon of liberal democracy, but just two minutes' reflection exposes them as corrupt organisations fronted by compromised politicians, spreading so much noise and confusion around the electoral process that democracy is left battered and bruised.

PRINCIPLE 12: Political parties should be abolished.

A commonly heard defence of party-based democracy is that there's no better alternative on offer. No longer...

In With The New

Having swept religions, political parties and nation-states out of the way, annulled their claims on the Earth and pulled the rug of power from under the feet of their proponents, we can now stand back and look at how the planet should be run.

It takes a while to realise the opportunities that would open up in such a world, opportunities for those with the weighty responsibility of managing resources, protecting the environment, keeping order, implementing justice, protecting human rights – in other words all the valid activities of government – without the complication of other-worldly authority, national and political allegiances, state frontiers and conflicting jurisdictions.

Structure

Imagine a world atlas with the 'political' pages missing. And on all the other pages – topographic, climatic, demographic, linguistic and so on – the political boundaries are missing too. All this land and sea, all these people to be protected, managed and allowed to flourish, without the messy, kaleidoscopic, illogical – and occasionally efficient – framework of countries, with their potential to corrupt every policy.

But it's not a new world *without* organisational structure we have to envisage here, not anarchy. Far from it. It's a world with a *rational* structure, a flexible structure that can react and adapt. A structure, in other words, that's fit for purpose.

*

First things first. Where the top level of governance lies depends on the subject area, i.e. the government service involved. For some it's the planet and previous sections have thrown up a few obvious contenders here: environmental protection, population management (numbers, migration patterns...), human rights, scientific research and so on. I'd add several more contentious ones too: security, education and taxation, for example.

Remember this group is defined by the geographical entity at which just the *top level* of jurisdiction should lie, rather than any suggestion that all aspects should be micro-managed worldwide by a global authority – the saints preserve us! Take education. I've suggested it in this category because I believe all children should have access to an objective, rational education free from religious propaganda and from sexist bias. The global education edicts may therefore focus more on *ex*clusions than *in*clusions. Which aspects of history and geography, for example, should be covered would quite legitimately fall within a more local jurisdiction. Likewise the age at which free education should start or end could well vary by local tradition or employment opportunities – and the practical question of school terms, days and times (should schools still be the means of delivery) would be an even more local matter. By the way, I'm using 'local' as a generic term to mean simply 'not global', regardless of the actual scale.

(In case the word 'edict' worried you, please keep a lid on your concerns until the 'Process' section below. I'm not eyeing up the post of World Dictator, not least because there'd be no such vacancy.)

Let's call these services where the top level of jurisdiction is a global one the **G type**. (*See*

Figure 1.)*

Which services do *not* fall within this category? An example would be road construction, traditionally the responsibility of a national highways agency, whose budget is at the mercy of a national government. Apart from a one-off global decision as to which side of the road to drive on (and our alien would be shaking his little antenna at the failure of politicians to achieve even this simple landmark of co-operation) and perhaps global conventions for signage and markings, there seems little reason why different regions on different continents shouldn't have the authority to build whatever roads they like, wherever they like and however they like. Similarly with new railways: subject to global standards of safety, environmental protection and of course guidelines in choice of gauge, railways could be built, opened or closed, double-tracked or single-tracked wherever the regional population decides they need to do so. Ditto, in principle, any other surface transport mode that pops up in the future.

Let's call those services like road and rail construction, where the top level of jurisdiction should be a local one, the **L type**.

---

*All figures appear at the end of the 'Process: Rational Democracy' section.

(Permitting, if you will, that L also stands for regional, continental or any other sub-global level.)

*

While on the subject of transport, it's worth taking a short detour to the relatively non-controversial service of air traffic control, in order to underline the practical advantages of removing states from the world map. While the requirements and conventions for air-traffic control even now come under a global authority (the International Civil Aviation Organization), in practice flights are passed from one Air Navigation Service Provider to another, which are overwhelmingly agencies of those states through whose airspace the flight passes: for example, one for the UK, another for Ireland and another (unfortunately) for France, giving its notoriously strike-happy controllers undue power of disruption. A 2015 report by the European Aviation Safety Agency cited the particular risk in Cyprus, where the ridiculous political situation on the ground (two republics on one small island: Cyprus and Northern Cyprus) has produced two air-traffic control authorities, creating confusion and potential danger above the ground. In the new world, air traffic control would definitely be a G-type service.

*

That's the top level jurisdiction: global or local, G-type or L-type. But, in the absence of states, what structure or structures would be appropriate for the day-to-day management of government business and the implementation of policies? Well, once again it depends on the service, and this time I'd suggest three basic types. (*See Figure 2.*)

The first is where government activity essentially involves supplying a universal service directly to the population. Health care, education, security and justice are all examples. From a structural point of view the key attribute is that the resources required vary with the size of the population, and so where population density is greater, more resources are needed per unit of territory. More ambulances in a thousand square kilometres of the Ganges Delta than in a thousand square kilometres of the Arabian Desert. This isn't rocket science. The organisational unit responsible for managing the service is therefore likely to cover a smaller territory in former Bangladesh than in former Saudi Arabia. (Only 'likely to', as experts in, in this case, health services would be needed to recommend the most efficient structure. I'm just guessing.)

Let's call these services whose supply is determined by population distribution the **P**

type. Remember these management categories are separate from the two categories, G-type and L-type, of top-level jurisdiction.

Another management category would be those services whose organisational unit probably needs to be territorial. A classic example is environmental management, for instance by river and water authorities. By and large, water supply and flood defences are best managed by river basin: the catchment area of the Thames (currently all in one state) or of the Rhine (currently in several). Although international co-operation is often successful, there have been instances of flooding in one country caused by government action upstream in another. Another example is management of forestry and control of deforestation over an upland area currently spanning more than one state. Weather forecasting also springs to mind. We currently have the ridiculous situation where the UK's Meteorological Office issues forecasts for only the north-east corner of the island of Ireland, the territory of the Irish Republic appearing completely blank on the map even though its weather is intimately linked to that over the border, because the Republic's forecasts are delivered by Met Éireann. How much money could be saved by simply having a single agency for the whole of the British

Isles?

Let's call those services whose supply is territorially determined, regardless of the population distribution, the **T type**.

There's a third category of service whose rational organisational units can be summed up as 'non-spatial', i.e. regardless of whether the top level of jurisdiction is global or local, a map is not a key tool in managing the delivery of the service. One such would be scientific research, naturally managed by subject of speciality and area of research, be it particle physics, genetic engineering, climate change or whatever. You could argue that it's organised in this way even now, but only with scope for interference by national governments – with their volatile funding priorities and a tendency to be diverted by the prospect of national prestige. Let's call such services, with organisational units unique to their subject matter, the **U type**.

*

So we'd have public services whose top level of jurisdiction is either G or L (global or local) and whose organisational structure is either P, T or U (population-related, territorial or unique). That's six category combinations in all: GP, GT, GU, LP, LT and LU. For example, education is GP, environmental management GT and scientific research GU.

Weather forecasting is LT and transport infrastructure (including for freight) probably LT, but public transport provision (for passengers) would be LP. You could think of a government service and suggest its rational category yourself. (One service I'm studiously deferring to a later section is security. Likewise, I'll cover the vital issue of language later as well.)

The result is a structure – a map of service delivery, if you like – that is not only rational but also *overlapping*. Gone would be the haphazard but rigid and suffocating structure of nation-states. While, for example, one city's education and health care might be supplied by two authorities with an identical territory of responsibility – the city-region – its environment might be protected by an authority covering a much larger area, including cities formerly in a different country. The environmental and health care authorities would naturally co-operate, but their top-level strategy and objectives, as well as their chain of command, would come from two different global agencies: a global environment agency and a global health care agency. For example, co-ordination of action to contain an epidemic, a phenomenon that knows no boundaries, would come directly from the top of the global health care agency to its relevant geographical units without interference from national governments.

*

These are just my opinions for a rational structure. You probably have different ideas. But the point is that, without state borders, *the opportunity arises* for designing a rational structure that's the most efficient, the most flexible, the most sustainable and the most effective for the people that government services are supposed to serve – you and me.

Process: Rational Democracy

In debates with naysayers, I find it odd that the opponents of a government operating at the global scale (which I admit seems to be the majority) almost always assume it would comprise a dictatorship of some kind and thus oppose the idea on principle without any further consideration. I think of them as 'globophobes'. Do they watch too many Bond films in which the arch villain sits in his (usually not her) remote fortress, planning world domination, the extermination of most of its population and endless supplies of high-quality cat food? If Hollywood could figure out a gripping plot featuring altruistic politicians, dedicated civil servants and wise old academics then maybe the naysayers would loosen their blinkers.

In Britain most of them also voted for the UK to quit the EU, one of the few polities to have successfully wrested sovereignty from the clutches of the nation-state. In justifying their stance, they'd often quote the so-called 'democratic deficit' of the EU (or, in the case of those *Daily Mail* readers for whom that's too tricky a concept, simply 'those faceless bureaucrats'), as though the UK were a beacon of democracy. If democracy is measured by how accurately the opinion of one voter in, say, fifty million is translated into one fifty-millionth of the influence on an eventual government decision... then the political processes of both the EU and the UK exhibit, as near as damn it, zero democracy. If you want to see such true democracy in action, you should visit neither Brussels nor Westminster but the cantons of Switzerland or some townships of the USA, where referendums are usually well planned, well understood and frequent.

The fundamental assertion of this little book is that a global level of government could and should operate democratically – or at least more democratically than the governments of most nation-states.

What, though, *is* democracy? If you suggested that democracy is all things to all people, I wouldn't disagree. This is no place to review centuries of debate on and experience of the subject – even if I were capable of such a task. The one study that made more sense to me than any other on the subject is John Burnheim's 1985 book *'Is Democracy Possible?'* (University of California Press). Having read it some years ago, I conceived of a 'democratic index', to which I alluded above in condemning both the EU and the UK.

It can be explained in two simple equations, defining ILI and DI.

$$ILI = (1/N)$$

where ILI is the ideal level of influence of a typical voter in a constituency and N is the number of voters in the constituency. For example, in a constituency of a hundred voters each should have one hundredth of the influence.

$$DI = (ALI / ILI) \times 100\%$$

where ALI is the actual level of influence of a typical voter in the constituency and **DI** is the **Democratic Index**. For example, if in the constituency of one hundred, a typical voter had only one five-hundredth of the influence (a large chunk of influence being held by a few voters or by forces other than the voters), then the Democratic Index would be 20%.

On this basis the Brexit referendum, for instance, should score a DI of 100% because each vote counted equally (a concept some politicians struggled to grasp), the Leave vote was greater and leave is indeed what the British government is in the process of doing at the time of writing – albeit rather falteringly and without much conviction!

But even in apparently squeaky-clean referendums, there are potential issues. The constituency may be poorly defined, excluding some people affected by the result and with a valid claim to have been consulted. The information presented to voters may not be accurate or even true. Some of the voters may be incapable of understanding the issue or the consequences of the options – in which case democracy may have been served, but may also not be a good thing (of which more later).

Referendums are examples of direct democracy, which even its most enthusiastic supporter would concede is never going to be a suitable method for day-to-day operational decisions. It looks like those bad guys over there are about to fire a deadly missile in our direction – what should we do? I know, let's arrange a referendum for next month and ask the people what we should do. I don't think so. Representative democracy has to be part of any practical system, not only to enable decision-making but also to link the government to the governed between votes. However, it's when assessing the Democratic Index of a representative system that the real 'noise' in the process becomes clear.

As pointed out above under 'The Party's Over', of all the issues on which the candidates differ, how does anyone know which was uppermost in the mind of any voter? Were all the issues even discussed? Are the candidates all independent or does each represent a political party and, if so, does each candidate agree with their party's stance on each and every issue? Of course they don't and so is a voter voting for the person or the party? Or are they actually voting *against* another party? If so, on what issues? In a 'first past the post' system, the influence of all the electorate who voted for anyone but the winner in any constituency (often a clear majority) is completely lost. If no party secures a majority, does the bargaining of policies for support reflect in any way the balance of opinion amongst the electorate? Who knows what that is anyway? Even if one party secures a majority and forms a government, is there a legal requirement that they implement their manifesto?

The list goes on. Every one of the questions above interferes with ALI, the actual level of influence of a typical voter in the DI equation. In Britain's case the interference is so great that ALI – and therefore DI, the Democratic Index – sinks so close to zero as to be effectively zero: on that definition, the political process is simply not democratic at all. In polities such as France or the USA where an elected president vies with an elected chamber for control of policy, the system is arguably even less democratic – if that were conceivable.

So in this rare opportunity I'm proposing, to design from scratch a democratic process for a world government – one that, if it proved successful, could be mirrored in the processes within levels of government below the global one – what's to be done? Practical representative systems aren't very democratic, but democratic systems aren't very practical.

Well, ladies and gentlemen... drum roll, please... there is a solution.

*

If it needs a name, **Rational Democracy** would be as good as any. It combines direct appeal to the opinions of the people with the deployment of their representatives in an effective way.

To outline rational democracy (and, to be truthful, there is only an outline) it's easier to step away temporarily from the controversial context of world government and instead imagine the people of an undefined territory of undefined scale and their need for a government to manage their public affairs.

The first question should be: What are their public affairs? I.e. that rarely posed question, as discussed above under 'What Is Government For?': Which areas should the government manage? This should be a matter for direct democracy via a referendum, with a list of subject areas (education, environmental protection, etc.) to be ticked or not, along with a reminder that, except for the unlikely scenario where voluntary service would cover it, a Yes means the service would be paid for from compulsory taxation of some kind. The architects of the referendum may well consider some that could be taken as read: is there any point in having a government at all if justice were left to hundreds of kangaroo courts? Anarchists are probably not reading this book anyway.

Who would be the architects of the referendum? Well, anonymous though this imaginary territory may be, its residents are bound to include some with experience of government and of management in other fields who could be appointed by the previous regime as a temporary 'Constitutional Committee'. These would preferably exclude previous party politicians, to avoid sliding back into bad old ways, and ideally include a number of previous civil servants. (Perhaps it could also include a nominal reader of the territory's equivalent of the *Daily Mail*, to note down these civil servants' names.) Incidentally, one of the pre-defined services not on the referendum list should be constitutional affairs and the agency supplying it, the Global Constitutional Agency (GCA), would subsequently replace this temporary committee.

The second question – or rather, series of questions – should be what is the overall objective of each government agency? If management of the territory's economy were one of the selected public services, what should the agency that manages it be charged with achieving? Full employment? Stable prices? Maybe, if only for old times' sake, even growth of total income should be an option. On a more practical level, what should be the aim of a public transport agency (if created)? Fares that cover costs? Accessibility for all? Painless commuting? Clearly some expertise would be needed on the constitutional committee to ensure that each potential objective is feasible. Moreover, the voters in any referendum would need to be given some idea of each option's cost.

The topic of expertise also arises in a more controversial way, for this stage of a rational democratic process – the assignment of objectives to government agencies – opens up the possibility of applying a feature to democracy that politicians have been studiously avoiding since universal suffrage arrived. While politicians may fear controversy, I have no such qualms...

PRINCIPLE 13: Voters should not

necessarily have equal voting rights.

(Stand back, readers, while the brickbats from the 'liberal elite' fly past your nose.)

How dare I suggest such a thing? Actually, it's not so daring. Are six-year-olds allowed to vote in elections? Why not? I've not heard of anyone answering this question before, but I suggest it's because their intelligence, powers of reasoning, knowledge and life experience are not yet sufficiently developed and the chances they'd vote for anyone offering free chocolate bars for life are pretty high. So the principle has already been established that some people do not have the mental capacity expected of a voter, in this case because of their age. But what about other reasons? At least in the UK, people with severe learning difficulties (or, to use the more accurate term, nowadays avoided, the mentally handicapped) are perfectly free to vote in elections and referendums and some do. I'm not suggesting that every adult shouldn't have the right to *representation* through a democratic process in which they have the opportunity to vote. After all, whatever the details of the system, the chances that a complete dolt will garner enough votes to win are slim – although, as you'll have observed, not actually zero. No, what I'm suggesting is that a *referendum* is a different matter. Here, it's reasonable to expect that any voter, whatever their opinion, will actually consider the advantages, disadvantages and costs of various options put before them and come to a conclusion via a rational process, even if that reasoning allows for prejudices that may be anathema to others. Alas, some people just don't have that rational ability. Others don't have the appropriate knowledge. This would be especially the case in the sort of subject-specific referendums I'm proposing, first for assigning the objectives of government agencies and subsequently for choosing between different policy options. For example, I'm no scientist and simply don't understand the pros and cons of developing GM crops. Should a referendum on this subject occur, I'd voluntarily abstain. More than this, I hope that I, along with all others wallowing in similar ignorance, would be legally excluded from voting. The same may be said for the allocation of funds between competing areas of scientific research: some of us are unquestionably incompetent on such matters. On the other hand, although my teaching experience is slim, I think I have a good enough handle on what compulsory, publicly funded education should and should not comprise and wouldn't mind a say on where my taxes are spent in this regard.

So how would such variable capacities among this imaginary territory's populace be assessed? Well, via tests of course. No one, but no one, gets an *automatic* vote in referendums. It's a matter of universal suffrage being replaced by *qualified* suffrage. If you want to vote in any referendum at all, you need to pass a test that assesses your rationality – or at least your capacity for rationality. (Whether you subsequently apply it or simply stick a pin anywhere on the ballot paper can never be checked.) Anyone can apply to vote in referendums, regardless of age, and everyone who passes must be open to regular re-testing. Beyond this, if you want to vote in subject-specific referendums, you have to pass an additional test of your knowledge or experience in that subject area. I'm not suggesting that economic policies, for instance, should be decided only by professional economists, but that they should be decided only by people who understand the basics of economics (markets, investment, entrepreneurship, taxation etc.) and are interested enough to want to vote.

(There's another alternative to universal suffrage called **sortition**, where small random samples from the electorate, rather like those called to jury service, make decisions or recommendations on individual issues after a short period of training and discussion. I've nothing against this version of democracy – indeed, it's based on groups likely to be more representative of the general population than politicians are – but it's not the subject of this book.)

*

The final piece in the rational democracy jigsaw, as viewed from this high-level overview, is representation. If government's role and objectives and even some policy choices are to be decided by referendum, what's left for representation? Would there be any role at all for those people whom we seem to be nudging ever closer to redundancy, i.e. politicians? Indeed there would: a vital role that guarantees life and energy in a system that might otherwise have seemed rather dry and almost robotic.

What are politicians? Wise people who see where the system is failing the electorate and with the drive and confidence to get something done about it. Well, that's the theory. So what turns so many of them into the self-serving, truth-bending, back-stabbing villains we witness today? Political parties, of course, as already discussed. The party machine that gives them the pathway to power soon tramples on their principles, changes idealists into liars and replaces any goals that may have driven them into politics with a single shared goal: power. Get into power and stay there. The party transforms politics from a moral calling into a ruthless sport: beat the opposition at all costs.

No parties, no party politicians.

In rational democracy a key role for a politician would be to identify causes in which he or she believes, argue the case for them, garner support and, if the cause is adopted (for example, via a referendum), stand for election as the people's representative to ensure the relevant policies are implemented. This is surely what most politicians set out to do until the party gets in the way. This is what politicians would be good at.

An example should make the process clear. In our imaginary territory there's a hot debate on what to do about congestion at its major airport. Business leaders are pressing the transport agency either to add a new runway or build a new airport, among them a Ms Greenfield who favours the latter. Environmentalists are urging them to do neither. A referendum is called, in which voters (those with the appropriate voting qualification) are asked to choose whether to do anything or nothing and, if the former, whether to build a new runway or a new airport. The agency has supplied estimated costs, benefits and the timescale for each option. The decision is to build a new airport. There follows an election to choose the person to represent this decision, to ensure the new airport is 'delivered' by the government. Among the candidates is Ms Greenfield, as well as other outspoken supporters of this option before the referendum and others who've come forward only afterwards. Ms Greenfield campaigns on her past experience in project management and her contacts within government and wins. She gives up her job in business and for the next ten years pushes the new airport project through, using her popular mandate both to bat aside frivolous objections from environmentalists and to hurry up any slackers inside government. Moreover, she becomes the public face of the project to all interested parties, including local people displaced by the construction site, and ensures they receive adequate compensation. In case anyone believes she's either overstepping the mark or even too incompetent to see the project through, a process is in place to review her performance and, if necessary, have her replaced through another election, which in any case would be needed if Ms Greenfield were to die while in her representative role.

Assuming she retains both health and competence, she completes her task and, with personal stock duly enhanced, decides either to return to her business activities or to adopt another good cause. Indeed there'd be nothing to stop her from taking up another cause during her time as new airport representative. For example, she may have noticed some serious flaws in the compensation process and begin campaigning for improvements, simultaneously becoming 'fair compensation representative'. However, the key attribute of these and similar roles filled by politicians is that they'd be time-limited, linked as they are to a specific one-off task. Let's call the job **Temporary Representative (TR)**. *(See Figure 3.)*

*

The other role for politicians would be as the people's **Permanent Representatives (PRs)** and to explain this we have to step back from our imaginary small territory and once again take a potentially global view. *(See Figures 4 and 5.)* A PR would be the link between a government agency and the people it serves. There'd be several – perhaps many – PRs for each agency. This is where representation mirrors the government structure discussed above (GP-type services, LT-type services and so on). For example, health services were suggested as a GP type: the top level of jurisdiction for health should be global and the organisational structure should be population-related. So there could well be, for instance, a single health authority serving all the inhabitants of Australia and another serving just the densely populated South Asian region of Bengal. The voters of each area would elect a permanent representative to the Global Health Care Agency (GHCA): the Health Care PR for Australia and the Health Care PR for Bengal. Along with hundreds of other Health Care PRs, these would form the permanent democratic input to the world's health service, both monitoring the activities and performance of the GHCA and representing it to their constituents. For example, the Health Care PR for Australia may well oversee the local distribution of a new vaccine developed by the GHCA.

Let's take a contrasting example: public transport, an LT-type service, where there's no need for a global agency (public transport being inherently 'local'), and the highest level of jurisdiction may include one authority for continental Europe. So there'd be a European Public Transport Agency (EPTA), with perhaps a dozen territorially based PRs: the Public Transport PR for Iberia, the Public Transport PR for Scandinavia, and so on. These elected PRs, each representing a territory of similar size, would keep an eye on the EPTA as a whole, as well as ensuring their own constituency got its fair share of public transport investment.

While these may be called *Permanent* Representatives, they would not, of course, be jobs for life. It's the job, not the person, that's permanent. Regular elections would be held, in which existing PRs could stand for re-election if they wished. What they could *not* do would be to form political parties with their colleagues in other agencies. While the Health PR, Justice PR and Environment PR for Australia may all be socialists at heart, the law would not permit them to form an official Australian socialist party, nor to stand for election under any name other than their own. Of course PRs would be liaising regularly with TRs in the same agency, probably passing on tips to their less experienced colleagues.

A Rationalist Manifesto

Figure 1 (opposite)
Rational Structure:
Top Level of Jurisdiction

G-Type Service (top)

Top level of jurisdiction is **global**.
E.g. human rights, environmental protection,
air traffic control.

L-Type Service (bottom)

Top level of jurisdiction is **local**.
E.g. road and rail construction.
There's no significance in the sample areas on
this map.

A Rationalist Manifesto

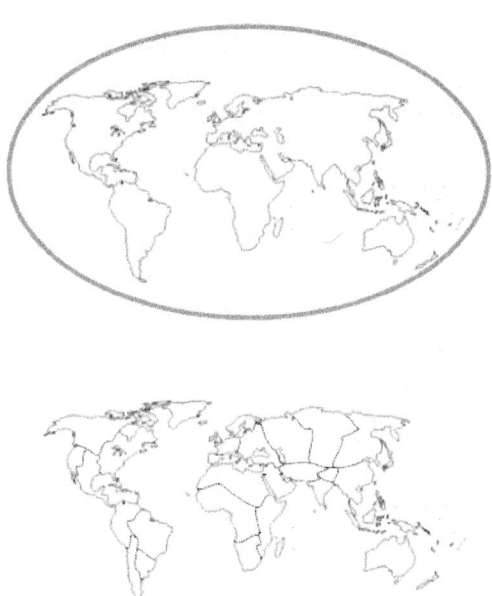

Figure 2 (opposite)
Rational Structure:
Day-To-Day Management

P-Type Service (top)
Supply determined by **population distribution**.
E.g. Health care, security.

T-Type Service (middle)
Supply determined by **territory**.
E.g. Water management.

U-Type Service (bottom).
Supply determined by **unique, non-spatial factors**.
E.g. Scientific research.

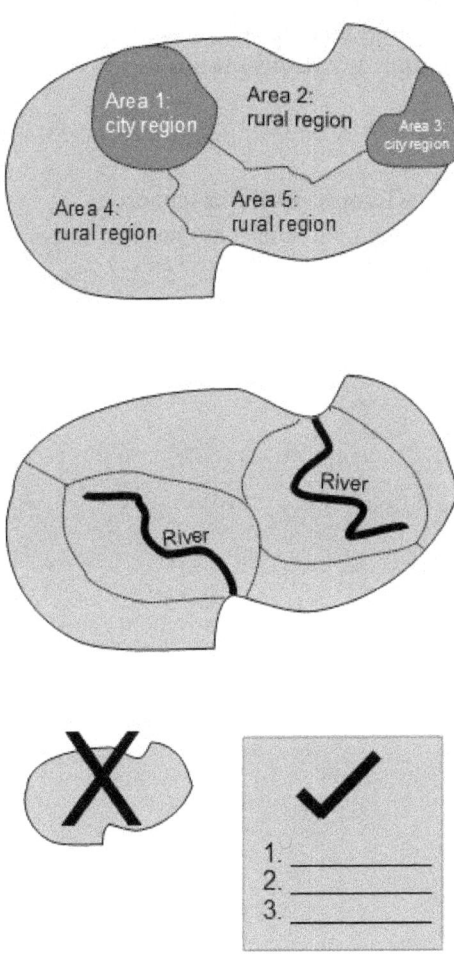

Figure 3 (opposite)
Rational Democratic Process:
Temporary Representatives

Example of one-off public transport issues in
Europe.
TR = Temporary Representative.
Geographical names are just territories, not
nationalities.

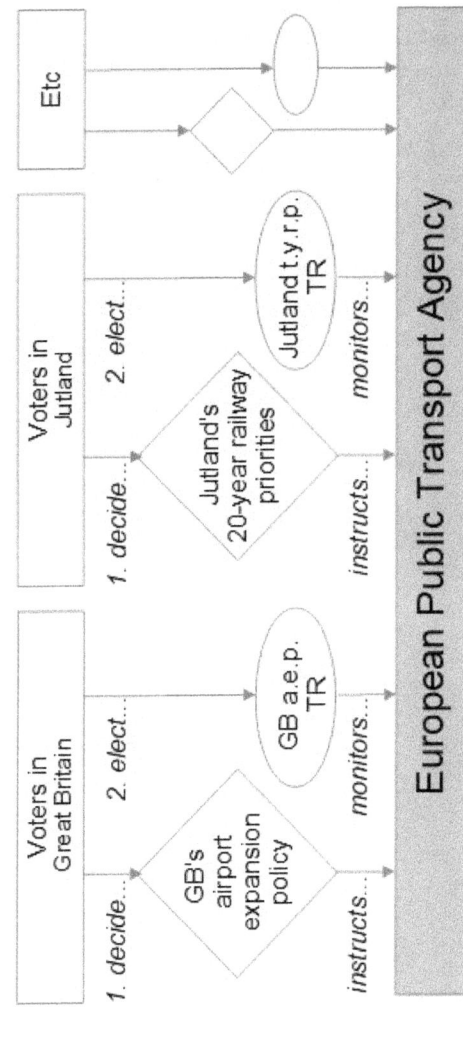

Voters in Great Britain

2. elect...

1. decide...

GB's airport expansion policy

GB a.e.p. TR

monitors...

instructs...

Voters in Jutland

2. elect...

1. decide...

Jutland's 20-year railway priorities

Jutland t.y.r.p. TR

monitors...

instructs...

Etc

European Public Transport Agency

implements policies directly or via local sub-agencies in GB, Jutland etc.

Figure 4 (opposite)
Rational Democratic Process:
Permanent Representatives For a G-Type
Service

Highest level of jusridiction **global**.
Example of health care.
HCPR = Health Care Permanent
Representative.
Geographical names are just territories, not
nationalities.

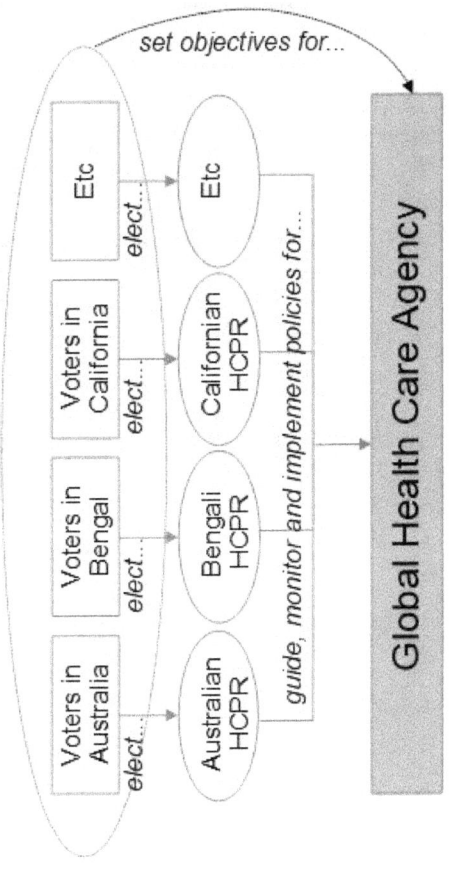

Figure 5 (opposite)
Rational Democratic Process:
Permanent Representatives For an L-Type
Service

Highest level of jurisdiction **local**.
Example of public transport in Europe.
PTPR = Public Transport Permanent.
Representative.
Geographical names are just territories, not
nationalities.

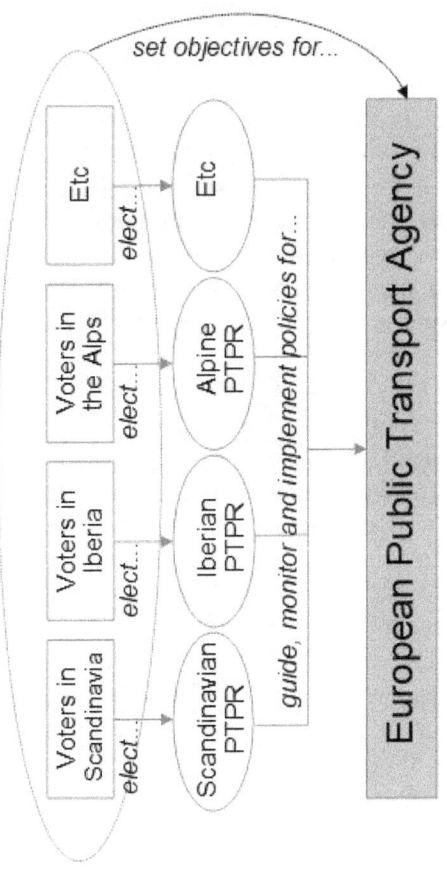

Jordi McGordy

Among the questions you may be asking (and doubts harbouring) about rational democracy, as summarised under 'Structure' and 'Process' above, two may be prominent: 1) How would this organisational kaleidoscope look from the point of view of an individual citizen? 2) A lot of elections and referendums have been mentioned – wouldn't there be far too many of them, soaking up huge public expenses and reducing the electorate to a state of exhaustion?

Let's imagine the rational democratic revolution has taken place (peacefully, of course) and the world has settled into a rational democratic political environment. And let's look at things from young Jordi's viewpoint.

Jordi McGordy is an imaginary thirty-something, born in Glasgow to a Scottish father and Catalan mother, brought up in Glasgow and now living in Barcelona with his Catalan wife and children. He's a medical doctor. When he was seventeen his parents encouraged him to take the citizenship test, which he passed, allowing him to vote in representative elections and in referendums not requiring any special qualification. In the

four years before he left Glasgow, he was
eligible to vote in twelve elections and five
referendums (a total of seventeen votes), did
so in all but three, but took part in only two
voting sessions. How so?

Well, in a practice that seemed normal to
many around the world, but which to the
electorate of the politically backward former
UK was a revolution in itself, both elections
and referendums were scheduled and
combined. Jordi's first session in Glasgow
occurred when he was eighteen. Despite his
youth, he preferred voting in person to voting
online and was proud to show the official his
photo ID as he entered the polling station.
Astonishingly even this step was relatively
new to the Glaswegians. After reading off the
qualifications against his citizen number, the
official handed Jordi four colour-coded sheets
of paper. These he took to a booth where he
settled into a chair for his first voting session.

The first, white sheet was headed
'Permanent Representatives' and comprised
four sub-headings as follows:

- Security PR for Western Europe
- Environment PR for Western Europe
- Transport PR for Glasgow region
- Local Services PR for Renton

Below each was a list of the candidates'

names, as well as a note advising voters when the next election for that particular post would be. Like everyone else, Jordi lived in overlapping constituencies. Like everywhere else, the constituencies had been defined on rational grounds, which meant most of them successfully avoided coinciding with former nation-states or other cultural/tribal entities. The higher the level for the highest jurisdiction of a service, the larger the population/territory covered by a single PR in that service. With the highest jurisdiction for both security and environmental services being the planet, each PR in that service had a pretty large constituency. At the other end of the scale, Jordi's local services such as street cleaning and rights of way were managed by a Glasgow-wide entity, at which his PR represented his own district of Renton. In between was transport, where the highest agency in Jordi's case was Great Britain (the island, not the shorthand for the former nation-state) and where his PR represented the Glasgow city region. So the permanent representation between Jordi and government wasn't just three or four non-specialist MPs or councillors, each representing a smaller and smaller area from state to district, but around twenty specialist PRs, each working with a specialist government agency at the top level and for each of which he had (or would have) the chance to vote them in – or indeed out.

Having assiduously done most of his research, Jordi quickly ticked the boxes against his chosen candidates for three of the roles, but left the Transport PR section blank, not having had enough time to compare the candidates. His parents – and the citizenship test – had stressed that no voting is compulsory and if he didn't feel able or qualified enough to offer a considered opinion on any issue or election, it was his citizen's duty *not* to vote.

Next he turned to the blue sheet, headed 'Temporary Representatives'. This comprised three sections, each once again with a list of candidates but this time also with a paragraph explaining the post. While Jordi briefly read all three sections, in only one did he tick a box. This section bore the sub-heading 'TR Following Referendum Decision R93/6002: Decommissioning of Nuclear Weapons'. Just before Jordi took his citizenship test, a global referendum had taken place in which all qualified voters were asked if all the old nuclear weapons technology of former nation-states should be decommissioned or if some should be retained for potential use by the global security agency in the event of an unspecified emergency. The vote had been overwhelmingly for total decommissioning. The post of TR to see this task through was a contentious one, as some of the candidates had historical links with the governments of former nuclear powers. Along with many of his fellow students, Jordi had strong opinions on this matter and now exercised his democratic right in the matter by placing his tick against the name of the Swedish candidate, a Nobel prize-winning chemist with no political background. All over the world, voters – some of whom Jordi knew as friends or family – were registering their choice on this same matter. What's more, online discussions with these and other contacts had, over the previous few months, helped him make up his mind on the matter and, as he made his mark on the ballot paper, he felt a frisson of pride that he lived in a world where millions of like-minded people could simultaneously and definitively make their voices heard.

For the other two TRs, both follow-ups to referendums in which he'd not taken part, Jordi decided not to cast a vote, on the grounds that he hadn't followed the initial campaigns and knew too little on the subjects.

Next he turned to the red sheet, headed 'Referendum: Global Constituency'. On this there was a single question posed by the

Global Education Agency (GEA), asking for a yes or no answer on the closing of a loop-hole in the implementation of a previous referendum decision to make religious schools illegal. The loop-hole involved teaching religion as a separate subject in a non-religious school. Should this also be made illegal? Another contentious issue on which Jordi also held a firm position. Another tick administered, another act of participation in the global community for the young man.

Finally, on a purple sheet headed 'Referendum: Constituency of North Britain', a question was asked under the auspices of the Global Population Movements Agency (GPMA), but applying only to a local constituency. The GPMA had been created to manage the upsurge in migration that followed the rational democracy revolution's removal of nation-states and therefore of national frontiers. Every human had automatically become a citizen of the Earth with the same basic rights as other humans, a situation that had taken *homo sapiens* only 200,000 years to achieve. Included was the right (but not necessarily the ability) to live anywhere they wished – with certain exceptions. These were areas protected for one reason or another and the referendum in which Jordi was about to vote asked whether he thought the highlands and islands of western Scotland should apply for such a status. It was another controversial issue, since many locals welcomed the incomers, whose presence made local services such as schools and hospitals more sustainable, while others thought the growing towns and suburbs were destroying the essentially wild nature of the area. Even the extent of the constituency for this referendum had been controversial, but in the end Jordi's address gave him the right to vote and once again he exercised it.

The voting session had taken Jordi about ten minutes; others who hadn't prepared as well took a little longer. He stood up, folded in two each of the four sheets so that his votes weren't visible and dropped them into the colour-coded ballot boxes. As he did so, he noticed that stamped on the back of his sheets was the letter E, for English. On the back of other sheets going in at the same time was a G, for Gaelic. Jordi's mother, who, with her Glasgow residence, was voting on exactly the same matters as her son, had chosen to vote in Catalan and was one of only three Glasgow residents choosing this medium in this voting session. Several more chose Spanish and many more chose Hindi. The vexed issue of language will be covered in a later section.

Leaving the polling station, Jordi spotted a

friend from college, an Asian student whose permanent residence for voting purposes was in Karachi, but who, on this worldwide voting day, was able to cast her votes in her own set of elections and referendums here in Glasgow. All the stewards needed was the citizen number on her photo ID to generate her own set of ballot papers. Although she could have saved them the time by voting online, she, like Jordi, was casting her first votes and really wanted to do so in person. The rational democratic revolution had galvanised young people to the extent that their percentage turnout actually exceeded that of older relatives.

Before he left Glasgow at the age of twenty-one, Jordi took part in just one more voting session, this time registering his vote on all the matters for which he was eligible. Once again it took him just ten minutes. Twenty minutes of voting in four years (plus as long as he felt he needed to research the background). Not too much of an effort for seventeen potential votes.

On obtaining his degree, Jordi got a place at a medical school in Barcelona. Although the crowded Catalan city was already one of the areas protected from unqualified migration by the GPMA, his educational place meant he had no problem getting a migration permit and made the move without further administrative intervention. There were no national frontiers to cross. His academic qualifications, as everyone else's, were valid worldwide and his citizen number granted him access to exactly the same rights as in Glasgow, including voting rights – except, of course, that the local referendums for which he qualified by residence were different from those he'd enjoyed in Glasgow. In fact, after two years, he qualified for an additional set of referendums based on a test that he passed on scientific knowledge and experience. The first scientific referendum in which he took part asked those with medical qualifications to choose between a number of research areas for the allocation of a significant tranche of funding. In this not only was the funding to be worldwide but so was the voting constituency – an example of rational democracy wresting suffrage away from merely geographical qualification.

*

Stepping back, it's worth examining what Jordi's story shows of the relationship between citizen and government under rational democracy, compared with that between citizen and state at present.

Under rational democracy, one citizen's democratic link with government, both global and local, would include their input to a series of decisions, in which there's no *a priori* reason why the processes shouldn't score 100% on the democratic index discussed above. In registering his opinion in a referendum, Jordi's ALI (actual level of influence) should be the same as his ILI (ideal level of influence), so long as you accept the system of qualified voting. A citizen's involvement in selecting representatives may score less than 100%, depending on how close the PRs and TRs stick to their manifestos, but at least there'd be no statistical 'noise' from political parties.

But democracy doesn't stop at election time. How would the citizen raise an issue with government between elections? In a traditional representative system, this would be via one of perhaps three all-purpose representatives, depending on the nature of the issue: a member of the national parliament, a regional councillor or a local councillor, each allocated to the citizen's constituency or ward. They probably wouldn't be experts in the issue concerned. Under rational democracy, on the other hand, the citizen would have a choice between three *types* of representative. The first, and most obvious, would be the 'local' PR for the service concerned: Education PR for an education issue, Security PR for a security issue, etc. That 'local' PR may be responsible for tens of millions of citizens, if the service were a global one, or for just a few thousand if it were a local one; but in all cases he or she would definitely have some expertise in the matter concerned. For example, if Jordi had a problem with the worldwide acceptance of his medical qualification, he'd contact the Health PR for Western Europe.

The second type would be a TR (temporary representative), if the issue concerned a particular project for which the TR was responsible. For example, if Jordi was having trouble getting compensation for property damage from a new rail tunnel under his Barcelona apartment block, he and his fellow-residents would contact the elected TR for the rail project.

The third type would be one we haven't yet mentioned: a Constitutional Permanent Representative (CPR). As previously mentioned, one of the global agencies would be the GCA (Global Constitutional Agency), which, amongst other things, would be responsible for managing voter qualifications and referendums and, like the other agencies, would be monitored by a body of permanent representatives. As well as their duties within the GCA, the CPRs would act as the default citizens' representatives for any issues that 'fall between the cracks' or for issues with the other PRs themselves. As such they'd effectively be the 'ombudsmen' of the system, the 'go-to' men and women when political trouble erupts. Mr McGordy, Jordi's father, who was old enough to remember times before the rational democratic revolution, regarded the local CPR as his 'MP'.

Political Power

In a rational democratic world, where would the power lie? Well, those whose knee-jerk reaction is to rail against any government at the global level doubtless imagine it would lie in the hands of a madman (or mad woman, I suppose – equality rocks both ways) thrust into prominence by democracy, only to bend the system to his or her autocratic will.

Maybe. Or probably not. And here's the thing: more probably not than in today's autocrat-friendly world.

In each government agency (for security, health, education, transport etc.), whether at global or local level, the relationship between the 'permanent' staff (civil service) and the people's representatives (PRs and TRs) would be along the lines of that in a democratic nation-state's government. With one important exception. The representatives would not be from a single political party or even a coalition of parties – because there'd be no parties. In fact, there'd be no government in the traditional sense. (Calm down, anarchists – it's not your turn now, or ever.) While there wouldn't be *a* government, there would of course be government – or governance, if you prefer. It's time to suggest how rational democratic government would work. And, to take the bull by the horns, let's look at the global level.

There would be, say, twenty agencies with jurisdiction at the global level: the Constitutional Agency, the Security Agency, the Human Rights Agency, the Environment Agency, the Health Agency and so on. Within each agency there would be several – perhaps many – PRs. Using the example quoted above, within the Health Agency there'd be the Health PR for Australia, the Health PR for Bengal and, say, ninety-eight more. These hundred Health PRs would elect one of their number to be the Global Health PR. Likewise there'd be nineteen other Global PRs, one for each of the global agencies, each an expert in their subject and each elected by their peers, each of whom would themselves have been democratically chosen by their local electorate.

These twenty Global PRs would form the key democratic body at the global level, the planet's 'cabinet' if you like. So let's call it the Global Cabinet (GC). In normal circumstances it would be chaired by the Global CPR (GCPR), the permanent constitutional representative selected from amongst the democratically elected CPRs. If our friendly alien had survived until after the RD revolution and felt obliged to make himself known to earthlings, speaking those traditional words 'Take me to your leader', it would be to the current GCPR that he should be directed. In emergency situations, the GC would be chaired instead by the PR of the Global Emergency Services Agency. The jobs of the twenty Global PRs being rather weighty, it would make sense for each, on election to the post, to nominate to their original local electorate a deputy PR to undertake their local responsibilities for the duration of their service. The duration of a Global PR's term and whether they could stand for re-election would of course be part of the constitution. It would, however, make sense for PR elections to be staggered, to retain some consistency and experience on the GC. (Remember: not only does the Global Cabinet *not* represent any party, it also does *not* reflect the result of any single, 'general' election.)

As to the permanent staff running each agency – the civil service – well, never having been a civil servant, I have no experience on which to base suggestions, but have no reason to think their way of working and especially their relationship with the people's representatives should be much different from the way they work around the world today. Two significant differences under RD, though, would be that their objectives would have been pre-defined by popular referendum and that there'd be no regular, politically motivated, sweeping changes, as there'd be no such thing as a change of government, merely a regular change of PR and the occasional instruction to implement a specific, democratically chosen policy, as monitored by a Temporary Representative. The staff of the Global Constitutional Agency would perhaps be the busiest, occupying themselves with voter qualification, the management of referendums and the drafting of legislation arising therefrom and from decisions by the GC.

The structures and processes at the global level, for agencies with a global jurisdiction, would be duplicated in each agency with a more local jurisdiction. For example there would be a South American Transport Agency (SATA) 'cabinet', comprising the elected Transport PRs for Patagonia, Amazonia, the Andean South-West and so on, who would have elected one of their number as their chair, the South American Transport 'Minister', as it were. With surface transport not having a global jurisdiction, SATA's goals, decisions and operation would be entirely between themselves and the South American electorate – subject to any edicts from such as the Global Environment Agency (on protection of the

Amazon rain forest, for example) or the Global Human Rights Agency (on safe working conditions for rail workers, for example).

What about the geographical location of government agencies, especially global agencies, global PRs and the GC? Well, as long as the internet works, there's no reason why they shouldn't be distributed around the planet, probably in a network parallel to the operational network of each agency. Nor would there any *a priori* reason why each agency's top management meetings, as well as the meetings of the cabinet, shouldn't take place by video conference – or an equivalent enabled by the technology of the time. The system should specifically avoid aggregating units of government in one location, to avoid the sort of resentment among less rational voters expressed in moans such as 'We don't want to be dominated by Brussels'.

But what if the internet, or any 'son of internet' fails? In this I do have some limited experience, which has taught me that the computer industry is peopled by specialists, each of whom know a lot about a little. There are so few who know enough about enough to unravel the causes of any catastrophic failure that I'm not convinced by claims for the internet's robustness. Just as under the current world order, a rational democratic world would have to be able to survive, if not necessarily prosper, without instant worldwide communication. Two of its features suggest it may have a better chance than the current, chaotic, nationalistic and antagonistic world. First, each level of each agency would already have its objectives set. And second, the military capabilities dispersed around the planet at regional and local levels would be small (compared with today's over-the-top 'defence' forces), being responsible only for maintaining order and responding to emergencies within their assigned territory. In other words, they wouldn't be equipped for aggression. (More on the security later.)

*

To summarise, political power in a rational democratic world would be *dispersed*. Just as with the EU's principle of subsidiarity, the power residing at the top of each functional agency would be at the lowest level for that function to be fulfilled. For those where this level is the planet, the power would be shared between a number of specialist representatives working with specialist civil servants. The representatives would co-ordinate (and, in the absence of party squabbles, one would hope also co-operate) in a cabinet, whose personnel gradually changes. The roles of the following cabinet members would be potentially more powerful than others: the permanent representatives of the constitutional, financial, security and emergency agencies. In order to prevent any one individual in any of these particular PR roles becoming too powerful, perhaps these agencies could always be represented by two simultaneous PRs from two different regions. Without the underlying hostility between political parties and nation-states (since both would have been abolished), the probability of peaceful and productive co-operation would surely be higher. Probability only, though: hostile and criminal activity are both aspects of human behaviour that can't simply be abolished out of existence.

There are, of course, other sources of power than political power. But this is 'just another *little* book'...

You and Whose Army?

There'll always be criminals and some of them will always be violent. A police force is always going to be necessary and will always have to include armed officers trained to deal with armed law-breakers. It may be that some of these violent criminals will always be terrorists, by which I mean people targeting the innocent in general rather than specific individuals, with the aim either of affecting public policy or of taking revenge for acts not committed by those targeted. There's nothing inherent in Rational Democracy – except perhaps its objective of weakening religion – that would inhibit any of these crimes, or reduce the need for security forces to protect the public from them and bring the perpetrators to justice.

Military forces, however, are a different matter. Since 2009 at least US$1.5 trillion per year has been devoted to military expenditure worldwide – and this excludes the more serious cost of deaths, injury and homelessness caused by military activities. Big numbers easily become meaningless. To put the one-and-a-half trillion in perspective, this is more than the value of the entire national economy of all but ten countries in the world. While it equates to 'only' about 2% of total world GDP, that 'only' is put into perspective by the fact that most 'developed' countries spend only about five times that on health care. In other words, for every five dollars spent trying to keep people alive another dollar is spent either protecting them from being killed by other states, preparing to kill them or actually killing them. Even this pales into insignificance beside the 25% of GDP that North Korea is rumoured to spend on military forces and which it believes protects them from the threat of attack, real or imagined.

For this is the background to all this military hardware, all those troops and (almost) all the activities they get up to. States have a history of attacking one another, of invading others' territories for the sake of resources, strategic value or simply their own prestige. According to one source[*], Britain alone has at one point or another been involved in invading 90% of the countries in the world. (Watch out, Luxembourg, you may still be on the hit list.) If at any moment any state isn't actually attacking another, it's probably threatening to do so or preparing to defend itself from attack, either real or

---

[*]See www.telegraph.co.uk/history/9653497.

imagined. (There are exceptions such as Costa Rica, which has survived for seventy years with no military forces, but very few of them.)

With Rational Democracy there'd be no states, no state governments to instigate an invasion, no state control of territory and no state-controlled military forces to direct anyway. Of all the rugs pulled from under nationalists by RD, the abolition of the state would certainly be the most important – and generate the biggest saving in wasted resources.

But would there be any need at all for military forces? Well, there'd certainly be two. You're probably itching to remind me that, in the twenty-first century, states are not the only source of military aggression. Rebel and terrorist organisations have been able to obtain military equipment and train willing fanatics to use them. While the supply of military equipment should be easier to control and monitor in an RD world, where security falls under a single command structure instead of more than two hundred, some would undoubtedly get into the wrong hands. Quite whom these 'wrong hands' would want to target is less certain, with no national governments to blame for perceived offences and no national citizens to threaten *en masse*. The most likely rebels would probably be those objecting to the former sovereignty of their own 'tribe' being replaced a global authority. (Step forward, The People's Front of America?)

The other valid legacy function for the militia would be the vital and praiseworthy role troops have filled in emergency humanitarian crises: natural disasters, famine, epidemics and the like.

So, after having removed their futile role in simply fighting each other, there'd still be work to be done by what are currently called 'military' forces. However, under RD there's no obvious reason why these resources and skills shouldn't simply be the heavy end of the police forces managed by the Global Security Agency. 'Police'? 'Military'? Simpler just to call them all security forces and place them all under the same command structure. (Thankfully the meaningless objective of 'national security' would no longer be amongst their responsibilities.)

Those globophobes immediately slipping into a paranoid state of fear at the idea of all security forces – local, regional and global – falling ultimately under a single authority should perhaps refer back to the 'Process' and 'Political Power' sections for reassurance on the democratic control of all RD agencies. They might also reflect on the obvious hazards in having two or more separate agencies, each armed to the teeth.

RD would offer the chance for the non-military population of the world, i.e. those potentially under the euphemistic heading 'collateral damage' in today's conflicts – me and probably you – to set the objectives and limitations for our security forces. These might, for example, restrict lethal activity only to that which would in all probability save more lives than it would cost, regardless of the 'nationality' of those lives ('nationality in this case referring to 'nation' rather than 'state', of course). No more pretence that American lives, for example, are worth more than Asian lives.

Using the New

This small book could be even smaller, by ending right here. But what follows are a few ideas on the types of policy that could be implemented in a world with the political structures and processes of rational democracy. Inevitably, they comprise a few pet ideas of my own, but the point is that any similarly radical policies could be proposed, democratically voted upon and, if approved, efficiently implemented across the appropriate jurisdiction.

Sounds boring? Depends on the policy...

Tower of Babel?

According to the Linguistic Society of America, there are over 6,000 distinct human languages in the world. Even the ten languages with the most native speakers account for less than half the world's population. It's a Tower of Babel out there. Even allowing for the fact that most people (about 60%) speak more than one language fairly fluently, these second languages are, of course, not all the same one. The result is that, 100,000 years after humans first developed spoken language, if you put two people selected at random into a room, the chances are they'd struggle to understand each other – and I count waving your arms about or pointing at a Google Translate screen as struggling.

Our friendly alien would be appalled. In fact, having assiduously learnt a few human languages himself before landing, he'd probably find himself helping a few poor earthlings understand what the others are so urgently trying to say. It might be "Watch out – it's an alien!"

And the difficulty people from different countries often have in communicating with each other isn't even the most extraordinary thing about languages. Incredibly, we're supposed to see this as good thing. So brainwashed are we by the 'diversity is good' mantra (see later under 'The Corrosive Cult of Respect'), that every minority language is treated like a dying patient who needs to be kept alive for as long as possible, whatever the cost. In fact the metaphor of death or of an endangered species seems to be obligatory when discussing any language whose use is falling. UNESCO even offers definitions for five categories of language: vulnerable, definitely endangered, severely endangered, critically endangered and extinct. And this is an organisation that spends millions of dollars on translations and interpreters. Some irony here?

There's certainly madness here. Languages are not animals. They are human inventions whose initial purpose was to enable us to communicate with each other, but whose effect in many cases is now to *prevent* us communicating with each other. Fortunately there is an obvious solution to this most profound of present-day problems. Unfortunately no one seems to have noticed it. It lies in the most encouraging of the statistics just quoted: monoglots (people who speak only one language) are in the minority. Learning a second or even third language is both common and easy. Easier still when you're young.

So the proposal is that everyone should learn at least two languages – *and one of them should be the same one for all*. Let's call it Language X. In this way, while everyone has the chance to use their local language, at the same time everyone can speak the same language. Isn't this obvious? Just think of the benefits of politicians and business people being able to negotiate directly and fluently, without the need for interpreters, and for anyone moving job or home to a new country. Even the relatively trivial activity of going on a distant holiday would be transformed. You arrive in a new territory – any new territory – pop into the first bar and immediately hear from the locals the latest news and their latest gripes, before instructing your taxi driver exactly where to take you, chatting to him about his family and yours, registering a precise complaint about your hotel room and settling in by the pool with the local newspaper. Or whatever.

And how would Language X be chosen? By referendum of course: a global referendum in which each voter has to answer just two questions:

A. What is your native language?

B. What is your preferred global language?

(B may not be the same as A.)

To get a simple majority for one language, the referendum may have to go through two iterations, where the first generates a shortlist of, say, two for the second. If this were done a few centuries ago, Language X might have been Latin. Two centuries ago it might have been French. Today it would almost certainly be English, of course. While English is the most common second language in over fifty countries, the next most common (French) comes in at only fourteen countries (note: countries as the measure, not people). In the not too distant future, such a referendum may throw up Chinese as Language X, which is already the most widely spoken first language.

Whichever it is, it should clearly stay as the officially adopted global language for some time, as declared in the referendum voting slip. Once identified, all children will learn it. Within two decades all young adults will be able to communicate with each other around the globe. Within a few more, everyone will. Isn't this a goal worth aiming for?

In terms of Rational Democracy it would not only be a tangible early benefit of the system, but also a key feature of its key processes. Except at local levels where a local language may be agreed, all meetings and

other communications between politicians –
PRs, TRs etc. – and between civil servants
would be in Language X by default. More
significantly for the ordinary person, the
default language for all communication with
government bodies – voting slips, tax forms,
hospital appointments etc. etc. – would also be
Language X. The savings compared to current
international administration would be huge.
The EU alone, representing less than ten per
cent of the world's population, is obliged to
translate documents into twenty-four
languages and employs over 5,000 translators
and interpreters on its permanent staff. The
most expensive of its languages is Irish,
costing the EU Parliament up to forty euros
per page. Under RD, the key word is 'default'.
Communications between government entities
and ordinary people would be free if in
Language X. All other languages (within
reason) would be available – but would be
priced at cost. You could ask for your tax form
in Hindi if you wanted (370m speakers), but it
would cost you. You could have it in German
(101m speakers), but it would cost you more.
Irish (less than 100,000)? Certainly, madam,
but you might like to check the cost first. As
we imagined above, Jordi McGordy's mother,
being one of the seven million Catalan
speakers, had decided to pay the fee and

therefore registered her votes in Glasgow in her native language.

Once again, isn't all this obvious? The answer, alas, is no. While I've presented this version of a possible future for the world's languages as an improvement, many people – probably most – would find it horrendous. They would actually prefer that people around the world (outside the spheres of business and science, which already use English as a global language) remain mutually unintelligible. They're willing to pay for the 'survival' of less-widely spoken languages, especially their own. What could be behind this attitude? There are at least two parallel answers: cultural identity and globophobia.

Language is a key feature of some cultures and in particular of some nations (rather than states). In shops, bars and on the street Catalans speak Catalan rather than Spanish (which all Catalans can also speak), not only because it's their native language but also because for years it was banned, under Spanish dictator General Franco. Just speaking the language is a declaration of their national identity. Who could imagine being French without speaking French, including all the shrugs and pouts? The proposal that under RD there'd be a global language, which probably wouldn't be Catalan or French, neither precludes nor seeks to prevent anyone from using their native language – or any other language – as well. In any case, a separate language, while a possible attribute of cultural identity, certainly isn't a necessary one. Chileans are quite distinct from Argentinians both to themselves and to the outside world, despite the fact that the dominant language in both countries is Spanish. Try telling a proud Scots woman from Edinburgh that, because she speaks English and not Gaelic (like 99% of her fellow Scots), she's not really Scottish. No, your identity with a particular nation, ethnic group or any other 'tribe' would not be inhibited simply because you can understand people outside the tribe.

Globophobes (people who fear anything at a global level) would indeed be alarmed by the concept of a global language. But so what? Aquaphobes (me, for instance) are unnerved at being in water, but it's our problem, not anyone else's. As with all phobias, there's no obligation on the rest of the world to adapt. The onus is on the phobics to get over it or accept it and cope. The world is already dramatically more globalized than it was a generation ago. A single official language is just a natural step that would adapt our lives to that fact, rather than forcing us to continually struggle against it. If you want to continue the resistance, go ahead, but don't expect us to pay for your translations.

There Are Too Many People. Full Stop.

At www.worldometers.info you can find the current estimate of the world's population, based, it says, 'on statistics and projections from the most reputable official organizations'. As I'm writing this it reads 7,526,869,663. No, sorry: 7,526,869,711. I glanced away.

We're all familiar with the graph of population over time that looks like a cross-section of half of Mount Kilimanjaro rising from the plains of East Africa: more or less level for ages before lurching into a steep upward curve around 1900 and continuing on a relentlessly dizzying gradient ever since. Some will also be familiar with the informative – and sometimes surprising – lectures by the late Hans Rosling, in which he reassures us that things are actually not quite as bad as they seem, since the current growth in numbers (and it's now 7,526,871,732 by the way) is the unavoidable result of past trends which have already changed and that the average family size in 'developing' countries has shrunk dramatically over the past few decades. According to Professor Rosling, the calming effects of more recent trends will probably pan out by, say, the end of the twenty-first century, when – barring catastrophe or new, unexpected trends – Kilimanjaro's summit should be approaching and the number of people on the planet should begin to stabilise.

So everything's all right then? Well, try telling that to a mother standing under a baking Ethiopian sun, sixty-fifth in the queue for clean water. Or a child competing with others for scraps of food in the Mumbai slum of Dharavi, where about a million people are crammed into an area the size of Chipping Campden. Or a Los Angeles commuter pulling up at the back of a mile-long traffic jam five lanes wide. Or even a shopper at Selfridge's on the last Saturday before Christmas. No, there are too many people. In addition, too many people live in the wrong place, while at the same time too many children are being born to those parents least equipped to see them through to a healthy, well-educated adulthood.

And here's the thing that would astonish our intelligent alien: there's no properly supported plan to sort this out.

Yes, there are local schemes to encourage demographically appropriate groups to re-settle elsewhere. Yes, plenty of agencies focus on spreading the tools for birth control or on installing equipment to purify drinking water or on developing all manner of means to help self-sufficiency. Yes, to a background of wailing nationalists, the admirable Angela Merkel even drummed up some support for a rational basis on which to distribute Syrian refugees around the EU. And one or two cities have been spurred into action in an attempt to restrict tourist numbers – Venice and Barcelona spring to mind; London doesn't, oddly.

But where's the overall strategy? Where's the UN definition of an over-crowded city, complete with subsidies to syphon inhabitants away? Where's the UN-issued permit for immigration restrictions? Where's the UN's plan to solve the shortage of economically active Russians by sending them millions of surplus Indians positively bursting with economic acumen? Where are the UN-imposed quotas for allocating refugees from war, famine and natural disaster between the countries that can take them? Where are the UN sanctions against those governments that actually encourage unsustainable growth in their population? (Yes, incredible though it may seem, France, for example, actually *celebrates* an increasing birth rate – presumably on the grounds that, whatever problems the rest of the world has, more and more little French persons must be a good thing.)

Where are all these global policies that follow from a global strategy to solve a global issue? Nowhere. There is no strategy. And the reason, of course, is that the juggling of policies on immigration, emigration, family size and overall population numbers isn't thought to be an issue that should be dealt with at a global level, but by individual states.

'Are you earthlings mad?' our alien may ask.

Yes, I'm afraid many of us are and many of the mad men and women who can't see a global issue even as it hovers in front of their noses are the men and women in power. This is not just my guess at their mindsets. In 2018 the Global Compact for Migration, acknowledging this as a global issue, as well as requiring co-operation by its signatories in an attempt to halt the surge in deaths from illegal migration attempts, was *not signed* by twenty-nine member states – even though they'd been among the full 193 states asking the UN to set this up two years before. The shameful twenty-nine included Australia and the USA.

Over-population is at the root of many economic, social and humanitarian problems. Unbalanced population distribution makes matters worse. This is a global issue that should be tackled by global policies.

Removing the 'Nations' from the United Nations

When the United Nations was formed in 1945 it was in the wake of two world wars that had not only killed millions of people but also left much of the globe in ruins and many of the survivors widowed, homeless or exhausted. The desire for a fresh start was palpable and the will of politicians strong enough to make something happen. Unfortunately – but inevitably – these politicians, even those with the vision to see the Earth as a single system, were national politicians, for this had been the highest level to which politicians could rise. And 'nation' of course meant 'nation-state'.

At its founding the UN comprised fifty-one member states; it now comprises 193. Membership is by state, structure is by state, political manoeuvring is by state and decision-making (or rather the lack of it) is by state. The General Assembly comprises 193 states, the Economic and Social Council fifty-four states and the Security Council fifteen states, of which five are permanent member states.

States, states, states... herein lies the UN's problem. For, worthwhile as is much of the work done by its agencies, in the end its objectives, its budget and its reach are determined and therefore restricted by the different interests of 193 'sovereign' states, as interpreted (or misinterpreted) by 193 national governments. Regardless of the multitudinous opinions and interests among the thousands or millions of people in each state, they are squashed into – or, just as likely, ignored by – the single view taken by that state's government as represented at the UN. And on the vital matter of security, the views of 178 of those state governments are potentially ignored anyway. And even among the fifteen on the security council, the stance taken by any one of five governments can block any action preferred by the other fourteen. And these five permanent members of the Security Council still – *still*, well into the twenty-first century – include two faded powers from the old world, France and the UK, while excluding giants of today's world like India, Brazil and the EU.

And, of course, by 'action', we mean simply 'resolution', i.e. merely a stiff note from the headmaster that can be ignored by its intended recipient. Resolution 2334 of December 2016 declared Israel's settlements in occupied Palestinian territories to be 'a flagrant violation' of international law. The Israeli government simply ignored it and carried on flagrantly violating.

As far as real political power is concerned – power to make fundamental changes to the world – the UN is toothless. A toothless, tuskless mammoth unable to protect its members from attack either by smaller beasts armed to the teeth or by the big bullies armed way beyond the teeth.

The obvious solution to this mess would be to remove the 193 states as members and replace them with 7,526,871,732 (or so) humans as members. From the United Nations to the United People. Except, of course, that we people are no more 'united' than the governments that purport to represent us – and never will be. The process to manage 7,526,871,732 (or so) opinions and convert them into rational and peaceful policies is Rational Democracy, as outlined above. The organisation to do this at the global level is not a United Nations but the series of global-level RD agencies outlined above under 'Structure'. The site of that UN tower block in New York wouldn't be a bad place to house some of their staff.

Despite its global scope and its good works, the United Nations is so hamstrung by its structure as an association of nation-states that it may as well be abolished under Rational Democracy.

A Less Absurd Economic Objective

Under 'Out With the Old', the case was made for consigning economic growth as an objective to the dustbin of history. With top-level governance at the global level, it's reasonable to ask what the over-arching economic goal for the Earth's population should be. Well, for a start, it should be democratically decided – and this in itself would be a giant leap forward from the growth goal of so many competing nation-states in the old world. But, for what it's worth, here's my suggestion.

While deaths from disease, accidents or natural disasters may never be eradicated, the premature loss of any human life, especially a young life, due to poverty in any its manifestations – hunger, malnutrition, lack of shelter, exhaustion – is a global scandal, a mark of the abject failure of the human species to care for its own. Poverty is an economic issue. Raising for everyone the level of either income or other financial resources above a minimum level, the level for survival in the relevant geographical context, should be the basic global economic goal. Any others – facilitating trade, encouraging entrepreneurs, managing markets and all the rest – pale into insignificance beside the prime economic goal: the eradication of poverty.

If and when this were achieved, many would direct their attention towards a redistribution of income to reduce the inequality they see as unjust. I'm not among them. (It's ironic that most of those who agitate for more income equality also applaud diversity.)

Differences in income and wealth are not only normal but beneficial, usually reflecting differences in effort, skill, talent or need that should be matched by different rewards. Clearly there are exceptions: for example, the absurdly high pay for top footballers, film stars or other 'celebrities' whose 'talent' is to do things of no inherent use. But even here those citizens who don't directly fund the celebrities could benefit from the out-of-kilter rewards through a suitably progressive system of income tax. There's no justification in criticising people simply for being successful. Significant differences in income and wealth are normal and desirable in a well-functioning, competitive society.

Where inequality is *not* justified is in the *opportunity* to become successful. While the two keys to opportunity are education and attitude, there's an argument that a third key –

the income and wealth of one's parents – is unfairly distributed and could be nullified by a simple piece of legislation: the abolition of financial inheritance. Simple in concept, but no doubt difficult in practice without a mighty effort to close all the loopholes sought out by thwarted parents. Perhaps the administrative effort to close the loopholes could be funded from the huge new source of revenue available to public policies when the default recipient of estates would be the public purse. Such a policy proposal, however, would probably become the most unpopular of all under RD and would therefore best be left until more voters see the light.

There's another potential global economic policy that would deserve more consideration. While there's little doubt that capitalism has won the battle with communism as the most efficient way to supply basic products to the masses at affordable prices, this doesn't mean that *unrestricted* capitalism is justified. In most of the world today, unless your product is positively harmful to its consumers without even the hint of a worthwhile use, you're at liberty to produce and distribute it either on the simple principle of free-market capitalism or, more indirectly, because it provides employment and tax revenues. Even under these conditions cigarettes and addictive video games, for example, seem to get through the net.

And there's the point: there isn't really any net at all. In most places there's no concept of licensing outside the industries of drugs, alcohol and arms production. This seems a mysteriously missed opportunity to improve the world. (Or perhaps not so mysterious given the preponderance of entrepreneurs among ruling elites.)

Why shouldn't anyone produce anything they like? One good reason is duplication. In the USA alone there are over 30 large motor companies and many more worldwide, most with vehicle models in the same categories. One family hatchback looks, behaves and costs very much like the next. Isn't the duplication between companies of expensive resources – designers, engineers, production lines, marketing departments, sales forces, support structures – rather a waste? How many motor companies does it take to keep the market competitive? Four? Five? Not hundreds. Another reason is simple pointlessness. Nowadays you can apparently buy a pet rock, a headband to hold your TV's remote control, a device to let you take your goldfish for a walk... perhaps the customers who buy this nonsense should really be spending their money on psychiatric care.

Enough's enough. Specifically, there are enough people in the world who actually need stuff that does useful things – and yet can't afford them – to allow this to go on. Under RD one proposal that may well find favour would be to introduce production licences. No licence, no business. A local panel would review every business plan with the idea of rejecting those viewed as absurdly dangerous or absurdly wasteful – or simply absurd.

All freedoms should have reasonable limits.

On Your Bike

Previous sections have raised the issues of unbalanced population distribution and of poverty. One policy area which might be used to alleviate both of these is social security – or benefits or welfare or any of the other titles covering policies that aim to boost the funds of those in financial trouble.

One thing should be made clear first: under rational democracy, the default responsibility for feeding and housing yourself and your children (and possibly your ageing parents) is you. And the default way to achieve this is through a job that pays enough to do it. But no redesign of the political landscape can include a magic wand to produce an exact match between jobs with job-seekers either in number or in location. There will always be a shortage of jobs somewhere and probably always a shortage of job-seekers somewhere else. Millions of people will always be out of work and unable to provide independently the minimum resources to feed, clothe and shelter themselves and their families.

Since both wealth and poverty will always be unevenly distributed by geography, this – and please forgive me for repetition here – is clearly an issue that needs to be addressed globally, even if the solutions are to be implemented locally. There needs to be a global system of short-term financial support that redistributes income from those with more than enough to those with less than enough. Yes, you the Christian New York stockbroker, will be required to subsidise the Muslim poor of Yemen; you, the Muslim Indonesian oil millionaire, will be required to subsidise the Hindu poor of Bengal; and indeed I, the comfortably-pensioned English atheist, will be required to subsidise the Catholic poor of Bolivia (darn!).

So far, so repetitive.

But a rational democratic world could go further. The financial benefits distributed by a Global Welfare Agency could be tweaked to shuffle the beneficiaries around. The unemployment benefit to which someone in a high-cost location is entitled could be set at the rate adequate to support a basic lifestyle in a lower-cost location. And not just a nearby one. Can't get a job in Reykjavik? OK, here's a subsidy to help you get a job in rural Turkey, where they're crying out for people with your skills. They all speak Language X over there of course. Your flight's all paid. Get your skates on (or rather off). Another tweak could help shift folks from over-populated to under-populated areas. Bottom fallen out of the film industry in Hollywood? The regional TV station in the half-empty Spanish province of Extremadura could use a few extra camera-operators. School class sizes could benefit from your children's attendance too. Even the long-term unemployed could be spread around to bring extra spending power to poorer areas. A global perspective to welfare payments, combined with a common language, opens up all sorts of possibilities.

The implications of a more mobile world on potential tensions between cultures will be taken up below in 'The Corrosive Cult of Respect'.

Show Us Your Money

Another policy that could oil the wheels of mobility is to give the Global Economics Agency the objective of achieving a single worldwide currency. Not just a globally accepted exchange medium like gold or US dollars or Bitcoin, but a currency that is so widely used for transactions of any size – from a few cents for a daily paper to billions of dollars for a company – that exchange rates from any rival currency are irrelevant.

In paying his way around the Earth, our friendly alien has been irritated by the constant need to switch between what he was appalled to discover are some 180 currencies – and that's just the official ones. How on Earth, he thought (literally), could the planet's governments have let things get into this mess?

Well, the answer is one that's becoming all too familiar: because they're national governments. Money isn't used just to settle debts but as a vital tool in the management of national economies. Not only the exchange rates of a country's currency, but also its money supply, its interest rates, its debt management and other tools are regularly adjusted as part of the country's monetary policy. This, its government believes, allows it to speed up or slow down inflation, GDP, investment – and all the other indices which it regards as important. 'Believes' rather than knows, because macro-economics isn't an exact science. But in the world of national politics perception is often more important than truth and if a government is perceived to be in control it will have a better chance of hanging on to power – which of course is its ultimate aim. Sacrifice our own currency? Never.

Well, almost never. Over the last two decades the European Union has implemented the brave project of squashing 19 of its national currencies into one, the euro. Following various financial crises within the eurozone, its critics have been quick to characterise the project as a failure and yet every day millions of people and businesses across those countries do indeed use the same currency. An odd definition of failure. Interestingly, in an authoritative book on the subject, Joseph E Stiglitz, former Chief Economist at the World Bank, puts the EU's difficulties in pursuing currency unity down to insufficient *political* unity. In other words, if the EU possessed all the financial institutions and powers usually associated with a nation-state (as well as the European Central Bank, which it has), it would probably manage a single currency better.

The doom-mongers who state categorically that a single currency is impossible across diverse economies based on, say, agriculture or oil or services somehow fail to notice that exactly this has been working for years in countries such as the USA, Russia or Canada, where different regions are indeed dominated by such contrasting economic activities. It all depends on what geographical area you define as 'an economy'. There's no *a priori* reason why, in the context of a currency, this shouldn't be the planet.

At least, in a rational democratic world, the electorate could be asked if it would like its economic gurus to be given the *objective* of creating a single global currency.

Who's Your Friend?

Each of us is born single. Most of us die single. If, between these events, we fall in or out of love with someone, live with them or leave them, what business is it of anyone else? Specifically, what business is it of the government?

There are two traditional answers. First, it's suggested that one of the bedrocks of a stable society is its recognition of a long-term relationship, potentially a lifetime relationship, between two people in the form of marriage. Fine. Let 'society' (whatever that is) recognise marriage in whatever form it wants – throwing flowers, dancing in the street, praising the Lord, exchanging vows, exchanging cows – who cares? This has nothing whatsoever to do with public administration.

Second, the couple may well have children and the responsibility of the parents for their children – and potentially of the children for their parents – should be reflected in law. Also fine. But what's needed for this is clearly not a marriage certificate but a parenthood certificate, i.e. simply a birth certificate signed by both parents.

Isn't this obvious? Obvious enough to put to the people in an RD referendum, I'd suggest. If in some parts of the world a majority decides it couldn't cope without the security blanket of legal marriage certificates, then let them invest some of their taxes in administering what, to the rest of the world, may be a pointless concept. With the proviso that it shouldn't be compulsory, of course.

Personal relationships are no business of government. Parenthood is.

(A positive side-effect of this would be to pull the rug from under homosexuals' complaints about inequality. No one marries. Happy now?)

The Corrosive Cult of Respect

A spectre haunts the world – the spectre of political correctness. Unlike the spectre of communism, which Marx and Engels regarded as positive, this one is seen as benevolent only by those woolly-minded left-wingers easily influenced by trendy Californians. One attribute of this 'spectre' is a strange semantic misunderstanding. Not as deadly as that between nation and state perhaps, but just as irritating.

The word 'respect' has two meanings. To respect someone's rights or expectations means to acknowledge they exist and act accordingly. To respect someone's opinions, or indeed the person himself or herself, means to hold them in esteem: quite a different concept. A simple example: the Flat Earth Society maintains the Earth is flat. We can respect their right to hold whatever opinion on the planet's morphology they choose, while simultaneously not respecting an opinion that clearly flies in the face of evidence. This distinction isn't difficult to grasp and yet the PC brigade seems to confuse the two meanings. When claiming the former they often erroneously demand the latter as well.

The context in which such confusion is most rampant is that of multi-culturalism.

As pointed out under 'There Is No God. Full Stop.', politically correct multi-culturalists try to persuade us that all religions are equally valid – while failing to notice that no religion is valid. From this they expand the idea to suggest that all cultures are equally deserving of respect and that the diversity of cultures on the planet – like the diversity of languages, discussed under 'Tower of Babel?' – is itself a thing to celebrate, protect and encourage. Well, celebrate away, you may say. What harm can it do? And what has this to do with Rational Democracy anyway?

That's the point, in fact. Culture*, multi- or otherwise, should lie outside the realms of public administration, of legislation and of services funded from compulsory taxation. In other words, so-called political correctness should, ironically, have no role to play in politics.

But alas, in many western countries, it has wormed its way in. Article 22 of the EU Charter states that the Union 'respects the

---

*Clearly, I'm using 'culture' in the everyday sense here, rather than the anthropological sense, in which all human activity, including administration, is 'culture'.

diversity of the cultures and traditions of the peoples of Europe'... and unfortunately this 'respect' has led to taxpayers' money being spent on official support for some of these cultures and traditions, especially those linked with minorities. Quite why the culture of a minority of people within an arbitrarily defined territory should deserve particular support is never explained. Well, under RD everyone will find themselves in a minority of some kind: the minorities will form the majority.

An irritating aspect of this corrosive cult of respect is that in many places making fun of any aspect of any minority culture is becoming a hazardous activity. In Britain it was only after considerable pressure that the concept of 'ridicule' was left out of the 'race hate' legislation that had the entirely laudable objective of making incitement to race-based violence illegal. If some do-gooders can't distinguish ridicule from hatred, perhaps they shouldn't be let out on their own. In France a law has been proposed that would render it illegal to make fun of regional French accents – a silly enough idea even without the inconvenient fact that all accents are regional in origin. Anyone in the public eye in a western liberal democracy brave enough to make fun of a minority – be it religious, racial, sexual, national or whatever – risks a severe backlash from the permanently offended 'snowflakes' on social media. In 2018 the leader of the British Labour Party found himself harassed and vilified because he maintained that criticising the Israeli government isn't necessarily anti-semitic. Woops, no: you can't disrespect the Jews, chirped the party's PC fanatics, unable to distinguish politics from race. He lost out and the preferred 'respectful' definition of anti-semitism found its way into party policy. At about the same time an ex-Conservative minister got hauled across the metaphorical coals for pointing out that women wearing burkas look rather like letter boxes – which indeed they do. The point is that all these issues are nothing whatsoever to do with government at any level. Ridicule and humour are perfectly valid tools in almost all situations – indeed, they're essentially what keeps the sane sane in this world. Rather than reaching for their worry beads, the appropriate response to the burka comment from the easily offended would have been to point out that the man who made it looks rather like a moving haystack.

Ridicule deflates egos. By all means show respect to individuals who deserve it, but whole races, whole tribes, whole nations? The two places where humour is currently most notably lacking are the Middle East and the USA. A religion that can't bear to look at an image of the person it worships is almost too funny to be true. A political landscape where the colours most commonly seen in newspapers – black and white – can barely be referred to as such for fear of accusations of racism, is so ridiculous as to be almost beyond a joke.

A rational democratic world should hold firm against such madness. Specifically, its governance should be blind not only to race and religion but also to nationality (in the 'nation' sense) and sexual orientation, meaning that it should ignore calls for any special treatment or protection on the basis of any of these attributes in the population it serves. Moreover, it should be made clear that being in a minority of some kind doesn't engender any sacred quality. Whatever the geographical level at which legislation applies, it applies equally to all people. The fact that your ancestors suffered at the hands of someone else's ancestors bestows no special status on you, or indeed on the 'someone else'. All family trees are populated by both heroes and villains. The past is the past. Rational democracy is about the future.

Sport, Culture and All That

A patriotic and law-abiding Chinese entrepreneur living and working in Rio de Janeiro will, through his income taxes, find that he's subsidising the Brazilian national football team. He has no interest in the game whatsoever, but if he did he'd naturally support China, not Brazil. A small portion of the council tax contributed by a low-paid care-worker in Birmingham is used to help fund the Birmingham Symphony Orchestra, although she has no interest in attending their concerts, even if she could afford it. Through his own local taxes, young Jordi McGordy (remember him?) helps the city of Barcelona put on a noisy, late-night celebration on April 23rd every year in honour of Sant Jordi. Even through double-glazing and headphones, the noise drives him to distraction.

These may seem trivial issues, but they're replicated literally billions of times around the world. Many non-essential public expenses are funded from compulsory taxation, taking money equally from those who happily contribute and those who don't. It's a mystery that the simple solution to such injustice, already mentioned under 'What Is Government

For?' hasn't already been implemented. (Perhaps it has, somewhere in the vast terrain of my ignorance.) The solution is to remove such activities from government responsibility and transfer them, one by one or category by category, to privately-run organisations, funded by voluntary subscriptions: the Brazilian National Football Association, the Birmingham Classical Music Society, the Catalan National Culture Club, and so on. It's not rocket science. Oh yes, the Russian Rocket Heritage Group.

In fact, perhaps it's not such a mystery after all. It's no coincidence that a majority of such organisations would probably have a national basis and be sponsored by those sharing a national identity. The adjective 'national' refers in this case to a nation rather than a state. While, under rational democracy, states would have disappeared, nations would of course remain, since these cultural entities are indestructible. And it's perhaps the current confusion between nation and state that explains why state governments, and indeed the populations they serve, simply assume that national cultural and sporting activities – non-essential, every one – should fall under the control of the state or of local government.

I can hear the wails from Arkansas artists, Bulgarian ballet dancers and Cambridgeshire cricketers even now. Without state sponsorship or council support, our clubs will collapse!

Perhaps. So what?

Appendices

The Thirteen Principles

This is a checklist of the principles proposed in this manifesto. More could easily be added, but perhaps these will generate enough controversy for a while.

PRINCIPLE 1: Gods are fiction.

PRINCIPLE 2: Government should ignore religion and spend no money supporting it.

PRINCIPLE 3: Any individual declaring belief in the supernatural should be barred from public office.

PRINCIPLE 4: Government funded by compulsory taxation should supply only those services deemed essential by a clear majority of the taxpayers.

PRINCIPLE 5: Economic growth, as an isolated aggregate statistic, should be dropped from all government analysis.

PRINCIPLE 6: 'Nation' and 'State' are two different things and should be treated as such.

PRINCIPLE 7: The nation-state is a bad thing.

PRINCIPLE 8: A system of public administration conceived, structured and run without the baggage of national identity and allegiance is a safer system.

PRINCIPLE 9: Monarchies should be definitively removed from the business of government and any that remain should not be funded by compulsory taxation.

PRINCIPLE 10: There's no such thing as an independent state.

PRINCIPLE 11: No part of the Earth, be it land, sea or air, belongs to any nation, state, race or tribe.

PRINCIPLE 12: Political parties should be abolished.

PRINCIPLE 13: Voters should not necessarily have equal voting rights.

Answers To Anticipated Questions (ATAQs)

This is all idealistic, isn't it?

Correct, thank you. Is there anything wrong with having ideals?

This is all too simplistic.

Simple, certainly. This is just a small book containing the ideas of a non-specialist in the field. But is it over-simplified to hide difficulties (a dictionary definition of 'simplistic')? Not by intention, but I'd be delighted to receive any comments from those wiser and more experienced. See end of the book for details.

You're trying to define a utopia where everyone will get on with each other and there'll be no divisions. This is unrealistic, isn't it?

Yes, absolutely unrealistic, but there's no such assumption. Quite the opposite in fact. Disagreement, division and disputes are the very essence of life and long may they continue. The purpose of RD's proposed structure and process (outlined in the sections of those names) is to manage these differences in a way that doesn't involve violence.

Rational Democracy sounds like 'one size fits all', when clearly it doesn't. For example, a Global Health Agency may decree that birth control is to be permitted everywhere, when many societies would strongly oppose it.

This issue – and the example quoted – go to the heart of RD. In principle, where 'one size does not fit all', the RD structure should reflect that, defining the top level of jurisdiction as somewhere below the level of the planet. But the example quoted is an interesting one, as access to birth control may be classified as a universal human right, regardless of the opinion of some (but not all?) in one 'society'. Just 'may be', because perhaps a majority of the global electorate in a human rights referendum would *not* approve this as a universal human right. How far liberal (or indeed reactionary) opinion penetrates would be something that the RD works out, rather than accepts as a pre-condition (except for the 'rationalist' principles listed in the previous section).

What's in Rational Democracy for me?

This pertinent question was raised by one

of the reviewers of a draft of this book. By way of example, he suggested the 'me' involved could be a Senitalese Islander, a Turkish Sufi or 'Disgusted of Tunbridge Wells'. A very good question in each case. Perhaps first it's worth remembering that RD is just the proposed system (structure and process), not the policies that may evolve from it. As with any change of system, some people are bound to object and indeed feel themselves worse off as a consequence. That's no reason not to implement it.

Let's take the examples one by one. Senitalese Islanders, probably numbering less than 200, occupy a small island in the Bay of Bengal, theoretically part of India but in practice completely isolated from the outside world because the islanders violently resist any approach by outsiders. This very situation, unlikely to change under RD, suggests that a world in which a significant majority wanted to change to RD wouldn't need the islanders approval. (It's worth stressing that they weren't asked whether they wanted to become part of India either.) However, while not the case in this example, other isolated communities may well benefit from RD, whether they know it or not. In removing power from such 'rogue' states as the USA, globally agreed action on environmental protection may, for example, inhibit rises in sea level due to global warming and, thereby protecting the territory involved.

What about the Turkish Sufi – someone who practises Islamic mysticism? This is easier. While he may gain in terms of a democratic input into matters that affect his region or locality, he will have a lot to lose. Since there's no such thing as god, there's also no basis in any mysticism, Islamic or otherwise. While the Sufi would be free to continue believing whatever nonsense he chooses (since thought itself is thankfully uncontrollable), one of the core objectives of RD is to undermine his ability to influence others. If a majority of the world's population still believes in gods, mystics or any other supernatural phenomena, there'd be no point in initiating RD.

As for 'Disgusted of Tunbridge Wells', I take this moniker to represent a stereotypically conservative middle-class Englishman. The key word is 'conservative'. If you don't like change – for good or bad – you won't like RD. Since Rational Democracy, by definition, could come about only via referendums, simply don't vote for it, D of TW. Eventually I hope you'll be out-voted.

Some of your policy suggestions –
excluding religious believers from office,

making no allowance for minorities,
suppressing political correctness etc. – reek of
intolerance. Isn't an intolerant world what
you're trying to get away from?

There's nothing in Rational Democracy that suggests religious zealots, diehard nationalists, unreconstructed monarchists and the like shouldn't be tolerated. They'd be perfectly free to to believe in and fight for whatever ideas they choose. But neither should they be protected from contempt or treated in any way differently from everyone else. The hope is that, when exposed to ridicule, ridiculous ideas eventually wither away. It happened with worship of the sun-god, the divine right of kings, racial supremacy, imperialism, male-only suffrage and all the other baloney that *homo sapiens* has ditched over the years. Why not the *bêtes noirs* exposed in this little treatise?

In voting, anyone would rather be one in
an electorate of seven million than one in
seven billion, wouldn't they?

In other words, democracy is always better closer to home? Well, surely it depends on the issue. If a worldwide agreement to ban nuclear weapons were successfully implemented, would you be happy that a small group of

Texans or Russians or Pakistanis could unilaterally – but democratically – decide to go ahead and build some anyway? If your own small group can make legitimate decisions, so can others. In any case Rational Democracy would allow for – indeed encourage – small electorates on issues that affect no one else.

Who would be in overall control?

For long-term strategy, the electorate. For short-term measures, the Global Permanent Representative (PR) of the policy area concerned, for example the Global Permanent Health Representative. In emergency situations, the Global Cabinet, chaired by the PR of the Global Emergency Services Agency. For more details see under 'Political Power'.

Wouldn't there be too much control?

There's no reason to believe so. Both in general and in particular contexts, there's a balance to be achieved between control and latitude. While it's true that with RD some activities could well be more controlled than without it (the availability of lethal weapons springs to mind), there's no inherent reason to assume this would be a significant trend. Indeed, the opposite would perhaps be more likely: the inhabitants of countries like Saudi

Arabia or North Korea, for example, would find their freedom of action much greater.

You're assuming the policies adopted at a global level would be the radical sort of which you personally approve. But they could just as well be reactionary or even authoritarian policies, e.g. Sharia Law.

This is an important point. As long as a majority of adults believe in a god of some kind, there'd be no point in initiating a shift to an RD world. Religion is absolutely anathema to the ideas in this book.

The suggestion of 'qualified voting', in which universal suffrage doesn't apply in every – or even any – case, seems ominous. Isn't this just elitism?

Well, yes. What's the problem with an elite if it's rationally selected and corralled by a pre-defined process? As mentioned under the relevant section ('Process: Rational Democracy'), the principle of restricting the vote by age qualification is already well-established around the world. My proposals are merely an extension of the same principle.

Surely the conditions required for Rational Democracy are never going to exist.

'Never' is a long time. The collapse of religion, the weakening of nationalism, the rejection of other tribal claims on territory – all these developments are theoretically only a generation away. Traditional, narrow-minded attitudes are not hard-wired into our brains but simply learnt from our elders. Attitudes can and do change. Within the last century ideas that once seemed unimaginable – equal rights for women, acceptance of homosexuality, widespread atheism, inter-continental travel for the masses, instant worldwide communication, instant access to most human knowledge – are all now commonplace. Raise your eyes, look beyond the horizon.

Don't we need alternative states to escape to if necessary (voting with your feet)?

Under the current system of nation-states, absolutely. Under Rational Democracy, there would be no states. There would, however, be territories where the local laws and policies on issues where a global jurisdiction is inappropriate are different from those in other territories. So it depends what you think you might want to escape from. If it's the local tendency to allow loud music all night, then by all means move. If it's the lack of freedom to indoctrinate your children with superstitious nonsense, then there's no escape, mate.

You present these ideas as original, but aren't they just the Swiss system writ large?

An excellent point. While I had the impression that I was suggesting the ideas bundled above in 'Rational Democracy' from scratch, it's true that Switzerland's political system does exhibit a similar mix of representative and direct democracy (i.e. referendums) that is both practical and apparently successful. I understand that Swiss citizens vote on about three occasions in an average year, each time answering multiple questions, posed in the context of both national and local constituencies. Moreover, the constitution is clear on how referendums may be called, which categories they fall into and what type of majority is required in each case. While not the only country to be so well-organised, Switzerland is indeed a political inspiration. I wonder if the Swiss are available for hire?

How would we transition?

A crucial question. And one to which I don't have the answer. Even with the best will in the world it's impossible to imagine that overnight billions of people would 'see the light' and especially that thousands of national politicians would happily forego the basis on which they'd risen to power. Short of a clean slate available to the planet's survivors after a catastrophic encounter with an asteroid, the only practical route to Rational Democracy would probably be similar to that followed by the European Union, i.e. the stage-by-stage assimilation of different countries democratically willing to 'pool their sovereignty'. The dangers of such a process are obvious: even if ultimately successful, an intermediate stage in which a huge RD bloc exists side-by-side with a bloc of belligerent, traditional (and traditionally belligerent) nation-states would be no safer – and possibly less safe – than the existing situation.

The honest answer to this question is: I don't know.

Anyway, is rationality a good thing?

People don't behave rationally all the time. For example, much has been made of the mismatch between traditional economic theory, which assumes rational behaviour on the part of an imaginary 'economic man', and the often haphazard and therefore unpredictable behaviour of real people. After all, every one of us does silly things now and then – and may not even regret it, cherishing the opportunity to 'let ourselves go'. There's no way in which any political system could – or should – inhibit this. One of the objectives of Rational Democracy, however, is to discourage irrationality in the boring but dangerous world of public administration, where I maintain rationality is indubitably a bad thing.

Is democracy a good thing?

Much has been written on this question and I'm in no position to add any new insight. Everyone has opinions. Any democratic decision is therefore likely to be regarded as the 'wrong' decision by someone. You could argue that policy-making by sortition, in which a small sample of the electorate is chosen at random and given the time and information needed to come up with the best decision, is another contender. But that would be another book.

References

Sources of statistics and other information, by chapter and sequence.

An Alien's View

www.un.org/sustainabledevelopment/hunger/
www.un.org/sustainabledevelopment/water-and-sanitation/
www.homelessworldcup.org/homelessness-statistics/
www.ploughshares.org/world-nuclear-stockpile-report

There Is No God. Full Stop.

www.adherents.com/Religions_By_Adherents.html
www.constituteproject.org/constitution/Saudi_Arabia_2005.pdf

Nation Does Not Equal State

The UN quote is from Article 1 of the UN Charter.

The King Is Dead. Full Stop.

https://en.wikipedia.org/wiki/List_of_current_monarchies

There Is No Such Thing As Independence

The Italian electricity blackout was covered at:
www.bbc.co.uk/1/hi/world/europe/3150788.stm

Process: Rational Democracy

Burnheim, John, *Is Democracy Possible?*
(University of California Press, 1985)

Tower of Babel?

www.linguisticsociety.org.
www.unesco.org/eu/languages-atlas
www.theweek.co.uk/eu/88088/eu-overspends-its-translation-budget-by-3m
www.vistawide.com/languages

There Are Too Many People. Full Stop.

The Global Compact for Migration was reported at:
www.globalnews.ca/news/4747488/un-migration-pact-signed.

The End of War?

www.sipri.org/media/press-release/2018/global-military-spending-remains-high-17-trillion
www.reinisfischer.com/top-10-largest-economies-world-gdp-nominal-2015

A Less Absurd Economic Objective

http://uk.businessinsider.com/biggest-car-companies-in-the-world-details-2018-2

Show Us Your Money

Stiglitz, Joseph E, *The Euro and its Threat to the Future of Europe* (Penguin Books, 2016)

The Corrosive Cult of Respect

'MP wants to ban sniggering at accents', *The Times*, 20th October 2018.

A Rationalist Manifesto

Colin Costa (not his real name) is neither a
politician, a journalist nor an academic.

Comments on the ideas in this book are
welcome:
Email: colincostard@gmail.com
Twitter: @ColinCosta1

For more copies of this book,
go to
www.amazon.co.uk
or
www.lulu.com
or
contact the author (see above)

A Rationalist Manifesto